Series in Computer-Assisted
Language Learning 1.

Teaching Languages With Computers

The State Of The Art

Edited by
Martha C. Pennington

ATHELSTAN

ISBN 0-940753-11-1 (cloth)
ISBN 0-940753-12-X (paper)

LCCN: 88-72268

Athelstan
P.O. Box 8025-W
La Jolla, CA 92038-8025
U.S.A.

Tel: (619) 552-9353

Contents

THIS BOOK IS DEDICATED to the memory of my father, Rohe V. Pennington, Jr., an engineer and inventor who left with me a sense of fascination with machines and with the elegance of mathematics.

Preface

While computers have filtered down into the K–12 grades only in this decade, computer-assisted instruction of some type or other has been in continuous use at several major universities since the late 1950's or early 1960's. Yet until very recently, most educators had no first-hand experience with or knowledge of computers. Not surprisingly, they therefore approached the medium as you would any unknown creature—conservatively, cautiously, and perhaps with a degree of skepticism or, in some cases, fear and hostility.

Though it may be true, as it has been said, that education lags a generation behind research discoveries and technological developments, those educators who have taken little notice of computers up to now cannot really be blamed for this. For the early applications of computers in post-secondary education bore as little resemblance to the typical classroom activities of the 1970's and 1980's as the early automobile assembly lines did to present-day self-directed work groups.

Like those assembly lines, the early educational uses of computers were intended to maximize efficiency by standardizing and mechanizing the learning process. In education, this was in some sense an idealistic and laudable goal, though it no doubt was motivated in the minds of the educational leaders of the time at least in part by the same "bottom-line" goals that motivated the early industrial giants. However, as in the case of auto workers, students were destined to fall far short of the goal of human-automatization.

It can be said that proponents of this type of computer-directed instruction were attempting to "correct for" individual learner tendencies which make humans less than perfectly efficient information processors—in a sense, attempting to make learning "learner-proof" (and "teacher-proof"). This was the kind of computer-directed instruction which until the last few years was the only type that many educators were aware of. Naturally, educators who lived through the last two decades were skeptical about computer-assisted instruction, as they would be about any form of instruction perceived as robotizing the student.

Some would say that educators are just now beginning to catch up to this influential technology and its potential uses in language instruction. Others realize that most educators have known about computers for a long time but have simply chosen to ignore them. For them the computer is new in the sense that they have been newly awakened to its potential value in their own classrooms. The significance of computers for them personally had before now escaped them.

The impression of computer-assisted instruction as new is the dawning realization among educators that computers hold promise for implementing many of the goals of the modern leaner-centered curriculum. What is being tried in education nowadays by means of computers, and what is being accomplished, is entirely different from first-generation uses, in terms of underlying pedagogical philosophy as well as in terms of implementations made possible with the increasing technological sophistication of the medium.

While a healthy skepticism about particular applications may still be warranted, no one in education can any longer refuse to be interested in the state of the art of computers, which, though changing more slowly in education than in some other computer-assisted fields, is nevertheless evolving at a rapid pace here too. It takes some work to keep up, and those whose knowledge was current five years ago would already be completely out of date in a number of areas of computer expertise, such as parsing theory, data storage techniques, and data processing by means of distributed representations.

This volume seeks to provide a relatively simple yet comprehensive update of the subject of teaching languages with computers, to help move educators into the next generation of this technology and its application to language pedagogy. It was hard to get the book written; it took almost exactly three years from the time it was conceived (May 1985) until the time it went to press (May 1988). Those three years were an important incubation period in which the volume editor and the other authors moved closer together in their ideas, and gaps in the manuscript, often reflecting gaps in our collective expertise, were gradually filled in. Had the book appeared earlier, it would have been in a very different—much longer and much less focused—form. The consensus is that in its present form, it is a much more interesting and useful book than in the original plan.

It has been a struggle to get this book out to the public, as very few publishers were willing at that time to take a chance on a "second-generation" computer book, especially one edited by someone who was not very well-known in the field of computers. There is no possibility of recouping the time and money spent in preparation costs. But this is of little importance if the book achieves its purpose, which is to open the eyes of even a small number of interested people to the resources that are available and, most importantly, to what could, with a little imagination, be done with computers in language education.

The volume is not in any sense a how-to book; teachers looking for "tips and techniques" are not likely to find them here. This is not an idea-book in that sense. It is rather essentially a concept-book, and for anyone willing to spend the time, it is a rich source not of the little ideas that teachers can try out in tomorrow's class, but of the big ideas that can shape educational curricula.

My grateful thanks go to Michael Barlow of Athelstan for believing in the project, putting his money where his mouth was, and helping to bring it to completion in a timely and professional manner. I also want to thank Carol Chapelle and Vance Stevens for reading the entire manuscript and offering many useful suggestions. I wish to express my appreciation as well for the time and support of Frank Otto, of CALICO, who originally offered to publish the material, and to all of the authors who were willing to contribute to the book and who believed in it enough to stick with me all this time. Luckily, I found a few people who felt almost as strongly as I did that a book like this was important, and was needed.

– Martha C. Pennington
Honolulu, Hawaii

Overview

Martha C. Pennington

A great deal of attention has been focused in the last decade on computer-assisted instruction (CAI), both for home use and in institutional settings. While most people would readily grant the utility of computers for word processing, mailing lists, statistical and other mathematical computations, and a host of scientific and business uses, there are many who are skeptical about the possibilities for learning languages through the medium of computers. Even those who concede that computers are usable in language instruction may wonder whether they are especially useful.

This volume is intended as an assessment of the state of the art of computer-assisted language learning (CALL) and teaching. The aim is to overview recent developments, current usage, and future potential of computers in language education in order to provide a perspective for administrators and teachers wondering whether to expend time and money for starting, maintaining, or expanding computer-assisted instructional programs. The overview is meant to be of value for those educators who have remained essentially outside the realm of computers, as well as for those who have had direct experience in computer-assisted instruction.

The volume addresses the technologies and techniques of CAI, while at the same time providing a creative vision of the potential of this marriage of technology, teaching, and learning in language education. It is thus not merely an overview of the craft of computer-based instruction, but is also a treatment of the art of CAI as it fits into the broader context of the language curriculum. The perspective of the volume is on technological and methodological advances in the present which will be guiding the next generation of applications of computers to language education. It is therefore a future-oriented volume, but the orientation is to the near future, the future that is already becoming in the present.

The book is divided into seven complementary parts, as follows:

1. Technology
2. Courseware
3. Research

4. Reading
5. Writing
6. Speaking/Listening
7. Program Development

For those with little or no computer experience, a background chapter (Chapter 1) provides definitions of terms and descriptions of technology and concepts underlying the discussion in the rest of the book. The next two chapters, which will be of interest to novices as well as to those experienced in CAI, provide a theoretical framework for CALL. Chapter 2 places current CALL developments in the larger historical and philosophical context of language education. Chapter 3 situates CALL in the larger research context of second language acquisition. Following these three general chapters are three chapters which treat computer applications in the specific language skill areas of Reading (Chapter 4), Writing (Chapter 5) and Speaking/Listening (Chapter 6). The final chapter of the book (Chapter 7) describes the CALL development process in the context of a vocational language course. The volume includes a glossary of terms, an extensive bibliography, an index, and cross-references by chapter and section title.

These chapters have been solicited from educators with expertise in CAI areas of special importance to language education and have been written to reflect the state-of-the-art theme of the volume. On the whole, we have avoided mention of specific products and have instead presented descriptions of types of products or computer uses—many of which are still in development—consistent with this theme. We have also attempted to keep every chapter wholly accessible to the non-specialist. Each chapter of the book is a self-contained article which may be read independently of the other chapters. Nevertheless, the volume is an integrated whole arranged in a logical sequence of parts. Taken together, the chapters provide a basic overview of the field of computer-assisted language learning as it has developed and is continuing to develop in the decade of the 1980's.

Chapter 1 ("Computer Capabilities Underlying Computer-Learner Interaction in CALL") is a review of the capabilities and potentials of computers for educational uses involving language instruction. In their technological overview, Susan Young Dever and Martha C. Pennington describe in clear terms, with supplementary diagrams, the elements of computerized instruction. After a brief introduction to several well-known computer languages, the authors describe a wide variety of types of hardware available for computer input and output. The description is set in a context of assessing the feasibility of each type of technology for language instruction. Attention is devoted to peripheral devices whose operation can be coordinated with a computer to incorporate digitized and synthesized audio and video images into language instruction. Dever and Pennington conclude that future developments will depend on an integration of theoretical knowledge about natural language and technical knowledge about the computer to achieve the most interactive learning with the user.

In Chapter 2 ("A Direction for CALL: From Behavioristic to Humanistic Courseware"), Vance Stevens discusses how language learning courseware and uses of that courseware are becoming more humanistic. Stevens documents the trend away from behaviorist modes of CALL, such as tutorials and drill-and-practice, and toward using CALL in a variety of communicative and functional ways. The trend is discussed with respect to three principles guiding the development and selection of CALL courseware. These principles, geared to promote uses of the computer in ways uniquely suited to language learning, are that courseware should be (1) intrinsically motivating, (2) truly interactive, and (3) eclectically selected. In particular, the chapter presents current directions for use of the computer in individualization of learning, and in facilitating socialization and peer interaction.

Chapter 3 ("Research Trends in Computer-Assisted Language Learning") examines the research which has been conducted on the effectiveness of computer-assisted language learning. The authors, Carol Chapelle and Joan Jamieson, approach their investigation by way of a series of questions, each of which is taken up in turn:

- Do students who use CALL learn more efficiently than those who do not?

- Are there some lesson strategies that are better in general than others?

- Are there some lesson strategies that are better for particular learners?

- Do students like to use CALL?

- What kind of learning takes place while students are using CALL?

Chapelle and Jamieson emphasize the importance of individualizing CALL to meet the needs of learners who may differ in such dimensions as age, expectations based on prior learning experiences, ability level, cognitive style and attitude. Their conclusion is that the effectiveness of CALL materials can only be judged in relation to complex questions about lesson features, learning processes, and learner characteristics.

Chapter 4 ("Computers and Reading Skills: The Medium and the Message") is a comprehensive treatment of the use and potential of computers in reading instruction. The author, David H. Wyatt, describes computer applications as of three types: those which are identical or similar to educational paradigms applied in non-computer media such as textbooks; those which extend existing paradigms in an "evolutionary" way; and those which actualize the potential of the new medium in truly "revolutionary" ways. Among the evolutionary software ideas are computerized reading laboratories, courseware which has stored large amounts of printed text for work on higher level reading skills, and programs which help students to develop faster and more efficient reading. The more revolutionary changes in reading instruction made possible by the computer medium are the capability of calling up definitions and other annotations on the computer screen at will while reading; of modeling the reading process on-line, guiding the user step-by-step; and of interacting with computer programs that implement creative and adventure reading paradigms to create a story. In Wyatt's opinion, the computer is still a "new medium" in education whose vast potential has hardly been tapped.

In Chapter 5 ("Computers, Composition, and Second Language Teaching"), Marianne Phinney relates the widespread adoption of the process approach in the teaching of composition and of computers in writing. According to Phinney, research in the composing process suggests that non-native writers approach writing in a manner which parallels that of native writers. Drawing on research with native speakers and with students of English as a Second Language (ESL), Phinney concludes that the main benefits of computer-assisted writing which have so far been documented are: improved attitudes toward language, toward the task of writing, and toward the student's own writing products; increased motivation to write, and so increased time spent in writing. The author suggests ways that the computer can be exploited in second language classes for pre-writing activities of various sorts, modelling and facilitating the writing process using simple word processors, productivity software, and process-prompting programs. The benefits of using the computer laboratory as a writing workshop are outlined, and some practical suggestions for implementing a computer-aided writing program are offered.

Chapter 6 ("Applications of Computers in the Development of Speaking and Listening Proficiency") is a characterization of the various aspects of speaking and listening proficiency and how the acquisition of oral and aural skills can be facilitated by computers. Martha C. Pennington depicts the computer as having the function of creating environments for meaningful interaction, as well as providing training in mechanical aspects of production and perception. Pennington explores ways of working on the different aspects of speaking and listening proficiency in group and individualized work through tutorials or language laboratory facilities. In addition to language practice and training, related applications involving testing and research are described.

Chapter 7 ("Designing Software for Vocational Language Programs: An Overview of the Development Process") addresses the practical concerns of a software development effort aimed at students in vocational language programs. Carolyn J. Keith and Peter A. Lafford review in some detail the steps necessary in designing effective vocational language courseware and highlight important aspects of the design process. Pre-design considerations include determining the time commitment that can be made, choosing the programming modality, determining the makeup of staff for the project, assessing needs, surveying available courseware, and deciding on the balance of vocational and linguistic content in the lessons. In the discussion of the design phase, the authors give suggestions for creating or compiling subject material and for programming the lessons to make the most effective use of the unique features of the computer and at the same time to meet the needs of the vocational student population for whom it is intended. In the post-design phase, topics addressed are field-testing and revision of the software, the writing of user documentation, dissemination of the courseware, and integration of the

CAI into classroom activities. The chapter includes useful illustrative material and concrete information about the decision-making process in a courseware development project.

The authors of these seven selections contribute much to the discussion of the question of how computers might make a valuable contribution to a language learning program. A wide variety of types of computer-centered and computer-aided learning are described, with attention to the related areas of research and assessment. Factors that can influence the outcome—and hence the success or failure—of computer-assisted instruction are identified and carefully examined in the light of the concrete realities of courseware development and the practical concerns of educators.

In their attitudes towards CAI, and towards CALL in particular, the authors range from optimistic to enthusiastic. At the same time, the general consensus is that we are still a long way from knowing the optimal combinations of computers, users and learning environments which result in effective language learning. Yet the authors do not share the view of some that the heyday of computers in language education has already come and gone. In fact, the sense of the volume is that the most exciting advances in CAI are just around the corner and that the field of computer-assisted language learning is just beginning to reach its stride. Only the next decade can tell us whether this promising technological medium will manage to realize all of the potential that is claimed for it in the present volume.

The Authors

CAROL CHAPELLE is an assistant professor of English as a Second Language at Iowa State University, where she develops courseware, conducts research on the use of computers for instruction of limited English speakers, and teaches courses on computers, language learning, and linguistics. She has published articles on computers and language learning and has served on the editorial board of *TESOL Quarterly.*

SUSAN YOUNG DEVER coordinates computer-assisted language learning at the University of Southern California, where she develops courseware and administers a computer-assisted instructional laboratory. She has published articles on computers and the teaching of reading, and she formerly served as audiovisual coordinator for the American Language Institute, University of Southern California.

JOAN JAMIESON is an assistant professor of English at Northern Arizona University. She was formerly with the University of Illinois, where she helped to develop and administer courseware on the PLATO system. She lectures and publishes articles on computer-assisted instruction and its effectiveness for different populations of language learners.

CAROLYN J. KEITH directed the Vocational English as a Second Language Curriculum Project at Maricopa Community Colleges, Phoenix, Arizona, during the two years that it produced computer-assisted instruction for limited English proficient vocational students. She is currently developing computer-based training in management systems.

PETER A. LAFFORD is the former coordinator of the Vocational English as a Second Language Curriculum Project for the Maricopa Community Colleges, Phoenix, Arizona. He has taught foreign languages and English as a Second Language in the United States and abroad. He currently consults in computer-assisted instruction and provides systems support for computer operations.

MARTHA C. PENNINGTON is an assistant professor in the Department of English as a Second Language at the University of Hawaii at Manoa, where she teaches and conducts research on the acquisition of second language phonology. She has given workshops and colloquia on computers and language learning and has published articles on the use of computers in research and teaching of second language phonology.

MARIANNE PHINNEY is the coordinator of the program in English for Speakers of Other Languages at the University of Texas at El Paso. Her experience includes work in both theoretical linguistics and English as a Second Language. She has conducted research and published articles in syntactic theory, second language acquisition, and the process of composing in a second language.

VANCE STEVENS is an instructional developer and lecturer in English as a Second Language in the Language Centre at Sultan Qaboos University, Oman. He was the first official chair of TESOL's Interest Section in Computer-Assisted Language Learning and has served on the editorial boards of *TESOL Quarterly* and *C.A.L.L. Digest*. His credits in this area include published software, articles, and bibliographies.

DAVID H. WYATT is the director of the Washington, D.C., area company, Specialized Curriculum Design, and a lecturer at Trinity College. He has been a featured speaker at conferences and symposia on computer-assisted language learning and has developed courseware and publications on this topic, including *Computers and ESL* (Harcourt Brace Jovanovich) and *Reading with Captain Yes!* (Addison-Wesley).

Technology

1 Computer Capabilities Underlying Computer-Learner Interaction

Susan Young Dever
and
Martha C. Pennington

1.1 Introduction

When educators are first introduced to computer-assisted language learning (CALL), they invariably ask how a machine, even one with the extraordinary capabilities of a computer, can assist a student in learning so human a skill as language. The answer they receive, whether positive or negative, is often replete with unfamiliar terms such as "artificial intelligence," "synthesizers," and "hard disk storage."

This chapter provides terminological and conceptual background for a consideration in later chapters of the general development of CALL instructional programs (**courseware**) and the application of computers to the design of instructional materials for particular skills or content areas. It does not attempt to convince the reader of the validity or invalidity of CALL. Rather, it describes various technical aspects of computers that are commonly applied to language instruction, in particular, those that underlie computer-learner interaction. The description is based on the assumption that the success or failure of computer-assisted language learning will ultimately depend upon the CALL designer's understanding of three interrelated factors: **language** as it is to be used by the computer and the learner, **software** to apply that theoretical knowledge about language in meaningful instruction for the learner, and **hardware** to produce and receive language in a manner comparable to human language use.

1.2 Language

Most people are aware that the computer is able to receive written language through a keyboard and display it on a screen or printed copy. The proliferation of calculators, computerized cash registers and word processors has guaranteed widespread familiarity with these standard methods of computer-user interaction. However, the computer clearly does not in any sense understand the words or data it is processing: it simply repeats operations, that is, it performs functions exactly according to instructions. Creating software that permits the computer to in some sense comprehend language and communicate meaningfully with the user is the subject of continuing research by linguists and computer scientists alike. As more is learned in this area, we can expect to see the development of more "intelligent" software.

Natural Language and Artificial Intelligence

Although the computer does not understand natural language, it is able to receive (**input**) and produce (**output**) tremendous quantities of data, as long as both input and output require only the manipulation of previously defined elements, i.e., items and rules for their combination. However, in order for computer-assisted language learning to be most viable, the computer should have the capability of interacting with the user in a manner approximating real communication. In particular, we might ultimately require the computer to be able to interact with the learner in a way that simulates natural language use.

A major barrier preventing the computer from developing the ability to comprehend and respond using natural language is the fact that there is as yet no comprehensive theoretical description of language and its use. Researchers in linguistics have provided partial descriptions of the structure of language and how this structure and its elements vary during use. Research in communication has begun to delineate the structure and the essential elements of the wider aspects of communication, including the non-verbal aspects. Research in cognitive processing of language has attempted to describe the interaction of linguistic and communicative knowledge with other knowledge and knowledge structures (e.g, **schemata** or **scripts**). Research in the three combined fields has advanced a great deal in the last decade but is still only beginning to yield results that can be applied to computer-assisted instruction of higher-level language skills.

Much of the effort in programming a computer to use natural language is tied in with research on **artificial intelligence** (AI). AI, in the strict sense, consists of software that causes the computer to behave in a humanly intelligent manner. That is, when the computer receives input it "knows how" (i.e., has been programmed) to initially process that input, to relate the input in a meaningful fashion to its previous "knowledge" (i.e., information in the computer memory), and to produce a meaningful response based upon the relationship. In other words, it **comprehends**, it **learns**, and it **responds**. AI researchers have found great difficulty in programming rules and data that come close to the vast reservoirs of strategies and information humans regularly, and often unconsciously, use in these functions (Waldrop, 1984; Winograd, 1984; Allen, 1987). The most successful natural language programming to date has been forced to greatly restrict the scope of the knowledge (i.e., the "world" or "universe of discourse") that the computer is cognizant of (i.e., the information upon which the computer operates). The restricted information with which the computer operates is often referred to as a **microworld**.

One of the earliest attempts to create a program that can talk to the user is **ELIZA** (Weizenbaum, 1976). In a scenario from this program called **DOCTOR**, the computer takes the role of a non-judgmental counselor who responds to the user's input in seemingly natural language. The apparently spontaneous response is accomplished by means of a keyword search technique in which the user's response is scanned and grammatically manipulated to form an answer (*"My mother hates me."* "Is it because *your mother hates you* that you came to see me?"). Certain keywords also elicit fixed responses. The keyword *machine*, for instance, elicits the question, "Are you afraid of computers?" Although ELIZA appears to conduct a natural conversation, it does not take the user long to discover that the program is only manipulating language—in a relatively complex way to be sure—but not in any sense comprehending.

SHRDLU (Winograd, 1972), developed after ELIZA, creates a limited world on the screen of colored cones, pyramids, and blocks which can be manipulated on a tabletop in response to commands. These commands are built from a limited vocabulary that includes words to describe the screen objects and their location. The computer **parses**, i.e., analyzes, the meaning of the commands, and this information is then related to what the computer has stored in its memory about its microworld. The program can therefore be said to comprehend the language of the input. **JOHN AND MARY**, part of the **GRAMMARLAND** program (Higgins, 1983), is a language learning program designed after SHRDLU. The microworld consists of two rooms inhabited by the characters John and Mary. The user can input questions and receive responses about the location of individual characters, can direct their movement from place to place, or can simply observe the machine carry on a similar dialog with itself (Higgins and Johns, 1984; Winograd, 1984).

These latter two programs are possibly the best known of the forerunners to artificially intelligent software. The techniques they used are among those most heavily employed in the bulk of commercially available software that purports to be "intelligent programming." The most capable of these programs (some of which fall into the category of expert systems described below) have been developed for use in specific business environments, such as inventory control and airline scheduling. It appears that it will be a very long time, however, before software is developed that will have sufficient command of natural language—i.e., that will be programmed to accurately generate and analyze creative language—to permit the computer to serve as a stand-alone medium of language instruction. In the meantime, most language learning courseware concentrates on teaching particular language skills and on using limited simulations of natural language interaction.

Two important approaches to "intelligent" software that hold much promise for the future are **expert systems** (Wilks, 1983) and **parallel distributed processing** (Rumelhart and McClelland, 1986). These two approaches have arisen out of attempts in AI, linguistics and psychology to accurately represent knowledge structures and the ways in which people access these in the process of comprehending and responding to language or other types of visual and auditory stimuli. The manipulation of data by an expert system is accomplished with reference to a stored **knowledge structure**, in a process that is meant to mirror human information storage and retrieval during comprehension. Rather than processing information **serially**, one unit at a time in sequence, parallel distributed processing (PDP) allows for simultaneous processing of small units of information and for connectivity among units.

The special features of the architecture and operation of expert systems and PDP programs, which have made them very attractive to researchers in AI and related fields, are also of value in the search for natural interaction in CALL. Expert systems are already being applied in the development of improved authoring systems and other types of CALL (Lian, 1987; Sussex, 1987). The applications of PDP to CALL have yet to be developed but surely cannot be too far off.

Computer Languages

Computer languages are artificial languages that have been invented to function efficiently in particular environments or to solve particular types of problems. **FORTRAN**, for example, designed for use by engineers and scientists, has a grammatical structure of formulas and equations, while **COBOL**, used extensively for business applications, is built of words, sentences, and paragraphs.

A computer language consists of elements such as symbols, commands and functions. The programmer combines these according to specific grammatical rules or processes, to create a program that performs a particular operation on a specified body of data. The distinction between computer languages and computer programs is not always clearcut. Users often purchase pre-programmed software, called **applications software**, that performs particular tasks such as word processing or data processing, but that also includes a limited programming language designed to be easy for the non-computer specialist to use.

Computer languages are designed to unambiguously express values and procedures and most utilize a relatively linear, left-to-right structure. This makes them suitable for problem-solving but fundamentally different from human language, which makes heavy use of redundant and ambiguous elements, in addition to a structure that permits embeddings to form complex clauses and sentences. Much current research in AI is focused on trying to duplicate these natural language properties in computers.

The "native language" of a computer is **machine language**, or **machine code**. It is a series of 0's and 1's, arranged in groups of 8 or 16 for most microcomputers, that the **Central Processing Unit** (the CPU, or computer "brain") can read and process. Different types of computers use different CPU's, and each has its own machine language. Since programs written in machine code are extremely long and very difficult for humans (non-CPU's) to read and write, a language called **Assembly** was developed. Assembly language uses a combination of mnemonics and numbers that directly parallel machine code but which are easier for humans to understand and to use.

After a program is written in Assembly, it is run through a **Compiler**, another program that translates the whole Assembly program into the machine code which the computer is able to work with. Although programming in Assembly language is difficult and must be accomplished by experienced programmers, the compiled Assembly program runs very fast and is thus used in applications that require exceptional speed and/or must process large amounts of data, such as voice recognition programs.

The most common language used in CALL programming for microcomputers is **BASIC**. BASIC is regularly used because it is easy to learn and because most microcomputers are sold with some dialect of BASIC included in the package. Although BASIC compilers are available, they are relatively expensive and are not ordinarily included in the computer purchase. Therefore, much of the BASIC instructional software (particularly the software in the public domain, which is not protected by copyright) is in a language called **Interpreted BASIC**. Each line of an Interpreted BASIC (or any other interpreted language) program is translated into machine code for the CPU as the program is run, in contrast to the whole-program translation method used by compiled languages. This line-by-line translation slows processing and occasionally results in unacceptably long delays for anyone using the program.

PASCAL and **C** are other computer languages that have begun to be used more often in designing CALL software. PASCAL was developed to help teach structured programming to computer science students. Its widespread use in computer science departments around the country and the recent appearance on the market of inexpensive compilers has resulted in a growing number of PASCAL programmers who are producing instructional software. The C language is less well-known in computer-assisted instruction. It is growing in popularity, however, partly because it runs faster than many computer languages without being as difficult as Assembly to learn and to work with. To date, C has been used primarily in **CAI** (computer-assisted instruction) to produce applications programs such as authoring systems.

Much effort is now being devoted to research and development in natural language comprehension and production by the computer. Two computer languages used extensively for research on natural language are **LISP** and **PROLOG**. LISP and PROLOG differ from the other programming languages discussed here because their structure, like that of natural language, readily permits **recursion** (Tesler, 1984), that is, building upon itself to form embeddings and complex constructions. However, to date only one dialect of LISP, called **LOGO**, has been used extensively in education. LOGO deals primarily with non-verbal mathematical and geometric concepts and is in widespread use in software development and computer literacy efforts aimed at elementary school students.

While natural language processing software is usually written in recursively structured languages such as LISP and PROLOG, it is possible to produce computer-assisted language learning software to teach specific language skills using any of the computer languages described above. In order to save time and effort, however, most producers of CALL courseware make use of one of the many authoring programs available.

Authoring Languages and Systems

An **authoring language** is a language designed specifically for producing educational software. An example is the authoring language **PILOT**, which many language teachers use to develop their own courseware. PILOT contains certain features that are especially useful in designing educational software such as branching to different parts of the program based on the student's answer. Instructional **authoring systems** are programs which aid in the construction of test or teaching materials and which require minimal programming on the part of the user. Authoring systems are generally easier to learn than authoring languages, which are in turn easier to learn than full computer languages (see Ch. 7, "Choice of Programming Modality," for further discussion).

Small-scale authoring systems allow people who know little or no programming to produce computer-assisted instruction by choosing among a limited number of options for constructing instructional or test items in such formats as true/false, multiple-choice or other restricted response formats such as story completion. The user then fills in the content text for each item in the format selected. Some authoring systems are large enough to contain elements of a computer language, thus making them more powerful but somewhat more challenging to use.

Authoring languages and the more sophisticated authoring systems are more difficult for novices to learn, but they permit additional flexibility in the design areas of:

- **screen display**, e.g., allowing for more attractive and complex graphics (visual images)

- **answer-judging**, e.g., accepting a wider variety of types of responses to a given test item

- **recordkeeping**, e.g., storing different kinds of student performance

- **branching** or **looping** to other parts of the program from a given point, which allows for variation in program content for different users and repetitions of certain items or item-types.

While authoring software can save a great deal of time and permit non-programming teachers to create CALL materials, all except the most sophisticated (and expensive) are limited in their ability to create language instruction of a communicative or interactive nature.

1.3 Hardware Input/Output

For Inputting and Outputting Text and Graphics

Computers have the capacity for receiving and producing many different types of input and output. The most common forms of computer output are text and graphic images on a display screen or **monitor**. Most microcomputers allow one to choose among various display modes that differ in degree of **resolution**. The mode of lowest resolution is **text** mode, which divides the screen into a matrix of twenty-four lines by eighty columns in the usual case. Text mode is used primarily for displaying **alphabetic characters**, although **graphics characters** that allow one to draw lines, blocks, and simple figures in text mode are also available for some computers.

In addition to text mode, most computers also include one or more **graphics** modes which allow one to access much smaller points on the screen. Each of these points can be turned on or off to create lines, letters, or pictures. In many systems, points can be assigned color as well. The graphics mode allows the user to produce more elaborate images than are possible with text mode.

As another form of output, the screen display or anything previously saved in the computer's memory can be printed out via a **printer**. A **letter-quality** printer, which operates much like a typewriter, prints symbols by means of a fixed **print-head**. A **dot-matrix** printer prints symbols and other visual images by arranging small dots on the page. Like the letter-quality printer, the dot matrix printer uses a ribbon to print. But unlike the letter-quality printer, it is not restricted to the characters of a print-head but can print anything—including complex graphics—which can be shown on the display screen.

The newer **laser** printers, which apply ink directly to a piece of paper rather than using a ribbon to print, have all the flexibility of a dot matrix printer but produce superior images. In addition, because they can apply ink to a large area of the page all at once, they are exceptionally fast printers. High-quality multi-color printers are now available which allow for color-highlighting of text or graphics in the creation of lesson materials.

Although the standard input device for the computer is the keyboard, many software packages make extensive use of alternative devices. These are sometimes incorporated into a CALL software package to permit the student to respond to non-verbal stimuli or with a non-verbal response, but they also serve as vehicles for inputting printed language responses or for implementing other forms of text-based or graphics-based interaction with the computer.

A variety of **special purpose keyboards** are available. Most that are used in language instruction have a small number of extra-large keys. They are designed for use by small children or by users who have motor disabilities. Another type of keyboard on the market includes a **speech recognition device** that will allow the user to mix limited spoken language input with text input.

Some computers offer the choice of **touch-screen** input. The user selects from text or pictures on the display screen by simply touching the screen at the place where the text or picture appears.

Another option allows the user to touch the screen or an external pad with a **light pen**. An external **graphics pad** allows the user to create images with a **stylus** and then input those images to the computer by pressing a button on the stylus. Some programs offer the option of creating a picture by combining stored graphics components via a keyboard or one of the other input devices. Special graphics software is also available for creating original orthographic characters, symbols, or pictures using these devices.

Two other common alternatives to the keyboard and the touch-screen are a **joystick**, sometimes called a **paddle**, and a **mouse**. The joystick, named for its similarity to what pilots have dubbed the joystick (a control lever) of an airplane, is a rod or handle which is attached to the computer electronically. The joystick can be tilted in any direction to direct the movement of the cursor, which positions the user on the monitor. The mouse is a small box, usually with a roller on its lower side, which is connected by a cord to the computer. It is pushed with the palm of the hand on a flat surface in any direction to move the cursor rapidly and accurately around the display screen. A less common device is the turtle, a turtle-shaped object much like the mouse but not designed to be held in the hand. The **turtle** is used with LOGO graphics to draw patterns on a flat surface as the patterns appear on the monitor and are input to the computer as a series of spatial instructions.

Joysticks have until recently been used for the most part only in recreational games, though they can be used in many ways with language software (see, Stevens, 1984, for discussion of use of game paddles in connection with English grammar courseware). Mouse capability is appearing in a rapidly growing range of software, including such textually-oriented programs as word processors designed for text editing.

These **keyboard alternatives** can be used effectively in CALL software to work with text as well as with visual images. The keyboard alternatives can be of value in language education both in making it possible for instructors to more quickly and efficiently produce quality CALL programming and in adding variety to the types of manipulations which learners can perform in using language learning software. Hence, keyboard alternatives provide a range of options for varying the type of interaction which the learner undertakes with the computer.

For Inputting and Outputting Sound and Video Images

Also of interest to language teachers is the computer's capacity for combining audio and video images (still and motion visual material from any source) with text (see Ch. 6 for applications of this technology in the oral language curriculum). There are three major sources of audio and video image production that can be incorporated into computer-assisted language learning software: direct audio and video recordings, direct recordings that have been digitized, and synthetically produced digital sound or images.

The first of these alternatives is computer-accessed tape recordings of source materials, such as audio recordings of a native speaker or video recordings of simulations or real-life situations. Several CALL programs currently on the market direct the computer to simply turn on and off an external audiotape recorder (via what is called a **signal converter**) at the appropriate moment during the lesson. It is also a possible to coordinate a sequence of slides or a video program via computer for use in classroom lessons.

Using this kind of system, the computer is not able to search back and forth for particular recorded segments or items, so that the system is unsuitable for use with instruction that varies, or branches, according to the student's response. The technology exists for a **branching search capability**, i.e., a capability of finding a particular location and then returning to the original point in the tape or slide sequence after branching, using an audiotape player, a videotape player, or a slide projector coordinated with the computer's operation. However, the mechanical process of searching from beginning to end of such media has proved to be unacceptably slow for use with most CAI.

More recently, **laserdisc** playback units have been developed which permit rapid access of specific audio or video segments within large bodies of recorded material. Laserdiscs, which are rapidly replacing more expensive and less efficient conventional videodiscs (note the spelling with c rather than k for laserdisc and videodisc, which are platter-shaped), can be made by transferring videotape to disc or by a direct recording using an optical memory disc recorder. Like ordinary records or videodiscs, laserdiscs encode audio or video information in concentric tracks. The data is stored in each track as a series of pits and unpitted areas whose pattern can be detected by a laser beam striking the disc. The light pattern of the laser beam is then converted into computer-readable input. While a few experimental units have been used to play back recorded speech or sound, most if not all laserdiscs today store data using the digitizing techniques described below (Lambert and Ropiequet, 1986; Lambert and Sallis, 1987).

Most commercially available laserdisc units now are limited to **read only** discs, that is, discs that cannot be altered during the process of working through the program. This type of disc is valuable in that it can play back video images which are synchronized with text. It therefore provides a medium for the development of lessons built around video images. However, it is limited in not allowing for any **write** capability—that is, the possibility of being modified by input. This limitation severely restricts the possibility of designing lessons which are at all interactive, since interactivity implies the possibility of manipulating aspects of the program. Units with **read and write** capability are in an advanced stage of development (Onosko, 1985; Helliwell, 1986). As the laserdisc medium becomes more widespread and the discs become less expensive to produce, we can expect laserdisc players to be widely incorporated into language learning software.

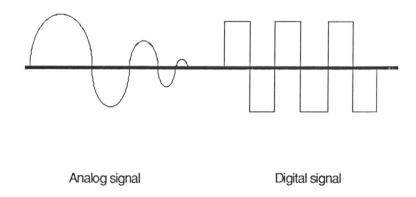

Analog signal   Digital signal

Figure 1. Graphic Representation of Analog and Digital Waveforms

A second method of incorporating audio and video images into CALL software is to convert recordings from the **analog** signal form of naturally occurring sound waves to an altered **digital** form. As can be noted in Figure 1, an analog signal directly reflects the continuous variation found in the source. A digital signal reflects a sequence of logical statements, most often expressed using the binary numerals 0 and 1. Most computers are digital computers and many signals that are originally recorded as analog signals are then translated to digital signals, or **digitized**, so that they can be easily and accurately processed by the computer.

As music lovers are now discovering, digitization can be employed to enhance sound quality in a recording, and digital recordings can be reproduced with higher fidelity than can analog. Digitized signals possess the additional advantage of being encoded in the same form and stored in the same manner in the computer as the code for the rest of the instructional software, thus saving time in retrieval. Digitized audio and video images can therefore be rapidly retrieved and reproduced or altered to suit the immediate instructional need. They can also be coordinated almost instantaneously with branching instruction, although the additional code required for digitization may strain the limited capacity of the average microcomputer used in education.

The process of digitizing an analog signal for language learning software can be summarized as follows:

1. A person's speech is recorded via microphone onto tape in analog form;

2. The recorded analog signal is converted to a digital signal by means of an **analog-digital converter** in a computer;

3. The computer then processes the digital signal according to programmed instructions;

4. The results of this digital processing may be sent to the monitor, a printer, or some other output device; or the processed signal can be routed back through the converter and then out of a speaker.

This is the same processing sequence normally used in digital music systems, such as **compact audiodisc** systems.

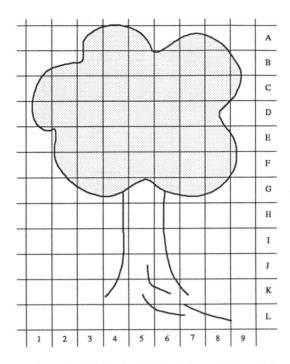

Figure 2. Sample Cells for Digitizing a Visual Image

Digitization can be pictured as a sampling process in which a grid is placed over an analog signal and sampled at each cell on the grid. Video as well as audio images can be digitized in this manner. When a picture is digitized, each cell may be sampled for the existence of the colors that the system is capable of processing. For example, if we digitize the picture shown in Figure 2, assuming that it is a colored image, cell C-4 might be sampled as follows:

red:	No
green:	Yes
blue:	No
intensity:	Yes
blinking:	No

Depending on the capabilities of our digital recording system, we might be able to identify other colors, mix the original colors to create different colors, and erase or add colors to alter the shape of the overall image. Of course, in true digitization the cells which are sampled are much smaller than is possible in our illustration here.

The digitization of prerecorded video images for use in language learning software is uncommon today, but it may be used more as the videodisc market expands.

Sound **waveforms** in graphic representation—e.g., as **speech spectrograms**, or **voice prints**—can be digitized in a similar fashion. Cells along one axis can test for the presence of **fundamental frequency** (vocal pitch) and **formant frequencies** (the characteristic pattern of harmonics of different sounds) and their amplitude (loudness). Cells along the other axis can test for the duration of the signal. Typically, in waveform digitization, duration is measured in periods of as long as one one-hundredth of a second for commercially available **voice recognition devices** and in one to several ten- or twenty-thousandths of a second for very high quality voice recognition and music. Here, as in almost every aspect of computer application, there is a trade-off between accuracy of analysis and representation of information, on the one hand, and sophistication and expense of hardware and software, on the other.

Video and audio images may also be created, or **synthesized**, through programming. **Synthesized video** can be produced by turning on or off specific points on the video display and assigning other display characteristics to them, such as color, degree of intensity, or flashing. Synthesized speech is produced with an additional piece of hardware called a **speech synthesizer** and its accompanying software. Instead of employing the waveform digitization technique, which requires a great deal of memory to store the high number of "samplings," an often used type of speech synthesis software encodes speech phonemically, that is, in terms of units of sound.

Phoneme synthesis is a process by which each phoneme, or sound, of a language is represented as a digital code, or string of symbols. This code is then translated by the synthesizer into particular patterns of frequency, duration and amplitude that model speech sounds. In this way, a program can produce relatively lifelike speech by stringing together codes which can in turn be entered as alphabetic characters via the keyboard (Ciarcia, 1984). Whether or not phonemically synthesized speech sounds realistic enough to serve as a language learning mode is a matter of some debate.

Computer Memory

Clearly, we are talking about vast quantities of data that must be stored when using digitized or synthesized audio and video. Schoen (1985) reports that he filled both sides of a double-sided floppy diskette with continuous speech in about ninety seconds using a type of speech board used for telephone communications in its fastest sampling mode. In its slower mode and using special data compression programming, he was able to increase the recording time to about five or six minutes, but with a reduction in quality of the speech output.

Some companies have tried to overcome this storage problem by marketing speech attachments for their computers. The now extinct IBM PCjr, for example, had an optional attachment for educational users, containing a pre-programmed chip—a small unit of circuitry adding memory to the computer—which had stored a few hundred words selected by educators to be most useful in an instructional setting. This attachment also permitted the user to record new words and phrases on a floppy disk. However, "a whole 360K disk could store [only] between one-and-a-half and three-and-a-half minutes, depending on the quality desired" (Badgett, 1984).

The large amounts of storage required for digitized audio and video images is in addition to that required by the possibly large amount of code in the instructional program. This program presents the lesson content to the student, controls the sequence of the content, and provides additional instructional overhead such as score-keeping and **utilities** (special subprograms or routines) to **config-ure** (i.e., adapt) the software and its content to a variety of educational settings. It is easy to see how the relatively limited memory capacity of even the largest microcomputers has placed severe limitations on the amount and quality of audio and voice synthesis that can be incorporated into instructional software.

The limited storage capacity of microcomputers is rapidly changing, however. In software, intense efforts are being made to develop more efficient data compression techniques. In hardware, **expansion boards** that permit the increase of a flexible type of computer memory referred to as **RAM** (random access memory) are now available for many microcomputers. The price of hard disks, which add permanent storage capacity to a computer and are now standard on many personal computers, has plummeted over the last few years. The smallest of these are equivalent to some twenty-five floppy diskettes in storage capacity.

New and much more efficient forms of storage, such as **bubble memory, pre-programmed ROM** (read only memory) chips, and **CD–ROM** (compact disc–read only memory), which have just started appearing on the commercial market, may soon become more widely available to instructional institutions. In addition, a new type of interactive compact disc, **CD–I**, that can store text, audio and video images of different kinds (see Ch. 5 for potential applications to reading), will allow for a quite extensive marriage of many of the media whose operation can be coordinated with the computer (Lambert and Sallis, 1987). This additional storage capacity together with new generations of microprocessors that process data faster make it probable that in the not too distant future digitized and synthesized audio and video will be integral to a wide range of instructional software.

1.4   Conclusion

Producers of CALL software are often forced to compromise between complexity and affordability. The more natural-sounding or natural-appearing the language and visuals employed by the computer in interaction with the learner, the greater will be the investment in terms of linguistic and technological complexity, development time, and dollars. Production in the future of more sophisticated and powerful language learning software will depend greatly on finding answers to questions such as the following:

1. **Language** How do the phonological, syntactic, semantic and pragmatic aspects of language interact in speech production and speech recognition? How can information gained from research in linguistics, communication, learning theory, artificial intelligence, and other related fields be brought to bear directly on the development of language learning courseware?

2. **Software** What are the types of commands and data structures for programming that most effectively simulate or directly translate into computer-generated natural language communication? How can a program be designed to most comprehensively meet the needs of language learning students? What languages or

programs permit production of the widest range of high quality language learning software?

3. Hardware What kinds of circuitry and electronic devices permit software to be processed rapidly and accurately enough to allow for spontaneous input and response that approximates natural language use? What storage medium permits the most rapid and efficient storage and retrieval of digitized/synthesized audio and video? What combination of input and output devices facilitates the highest degree of language learning among the largest number of students?

Although the computer is a comparatively new educational medium, particularly for language instruction, it is likely that many hardware and software questions will be either answered or moot by the turn of the century. The answers to questions about language may come to light more slowly. Nonetheless, the effectiveness of computer-assisted language learning will ultimately depend on the ability to integrate theoretical knowledge of natural language with a technical understanding of software and hardware to achieve the most productive interaction between computer and learner.

Courseware

2 A Direction For CALL: From Behavioristic to Humanistic Courseware

Vance Stevens

2.1 Introduction

Computer-assisted language learning, more commonly referred to as CALL, is a field whose recent development has reflected the exponential rate of change inherent in other aspects of computer technology. This change has been taking place against a backdrop of equally significant shifts in perceptions of how people learn languages, and in perceptions of who language learners are and what their individual needs and differences are. The shift of attention to individual needs of students, an important theme in this chapter, is taken up as a focus of CALL research in the next chapter.

This chapter characterizes the methodological stream of change as a factor affecting current approaches to CALL software development. In particular, I will examine how CALL software has, from its roots in behaviorism, evolved more humanistic and communicative applications to language learning.

2.2 Computers as Behaviorist-Based Teaching Devices

The first efforts of any significance in the teaching of languages using computers occurred during the late 1960's (see Ahmad, Corbett, Rogers and Sussex, 1985, for a thorough treatment) and for more than a decade, where computers were used in language learning, it was usually in ways designed to structure learning along the lines of behaviorist models then in vogue. Accordingly, **programmed instruction** (PI) was considered the optimal model for courseware design. Lewis (1981, p. 48) observes that because CAI was used originally to speed up the process of PI, it was resisted by teachers and "has not been a huge success." Also, in Rivers' (1981) treatment of CAI in the context of the many ways then considered effective for teaching foreign language skills, PI is the only modality considered. Indeed, Rivers' definition (p. 45) of "effective courseware" (i.e., "a learning sequence which is carefully designed and executed") would not characterize all courseware considered effective in language learning today.

The salient flaw in instructional algorithms based on behaviorism was the assumption that learning could be reduced to its lowest common denominators, and that teaching could thus most effectively proceed as a series of pre-planned discrete steps. Because programming is also a discipline in which the steps in a given task are clearly defined, it was tempting to conceptualize early CALL efforts along the lines of the behaviorist models. Drill-and-practice became the preferred (and the most effective, according to Vinsonhaler and Bass, 1972) mode of delivery, and this mode managed to stay in vogue even after pattern practice had fallen out of favor in language classrooms. Even then, it was thought that drill-and-practice software could somehow satisfy the students' need for the sustained, tedious (i.e., boring) kind of teaching that many teachers preferred not to do in class. Unfortunately, this did not prove to be the case. Although computers are often able to amuse first-time users for long periods of time no matter what the software, the novelty wears off, and student users do not, of their own accord, spend any more time with redundant and repetitive courseware than they do with the books on which such courseware is based.

Besides its failure to stay current with methodological trends in language learning, CALL courseware has typically exploited few of those aspects of the medium holding greatest potential for use of computers as learning tools (e.g., inherent recursiveness of operations or the ability to randomize). True, many of the computer's special attributes have been utilized with drill-and-practice courseware, such as its repetitive capability, its capacity to evaluate responses and branch accordingly, and the privacy and immediacy of its feedback (see Ch. 1, "Language," for discussion of these capabilities). These are valuable assets in an instructional medium, but they are not impossible to achieve in other media (a programmed text, for example). The situation was aptly characterized by Papert (1980a) as being analogous to the first efforts of film makers, who essentially staged plays and filmed them straight on, only gradually evolving the special characteristics and techniques which make experiencing a movie very different from watching a play.

Educators have likewise come to realize that computers, like Hollywood cameras, are best exploited in ways that take advantage of their particular characteristics rather than when they are used to try to "improve" deliveries in the media they seem to be replacing. In fact, cinema cameras and computers were only following on stage plays and books, not replacing them at all; plays and books have valid places in culture and education, and what they are good for need not be replaced. Thus, attention to computers in language learning is most wisely focused on those attributes which are most likely to uniquely facilitate that process.

2.3   Computers as Facilitators for Humanistic Learning

With the advent of the "personal" microcomputer in the late seventies, the realm of computing has come in a few short years to spread far beyond the walls of buildings containing mainframe computers. As a result, a wide spectrum of educators, many among them innovative language teachers, have been in a position to deal constructively with deficiencies in the software available to them. The majority of these teachers had long since revised many of the notions on which behaviorist-based courseware, such as drill-and-practice, were based, adopting instead more humanistic approaches to language learning. Before going further, it will be useful to examine what such approaches entail.

Over the past decade, there have been shifts in emphasis in language teaching from form to function and from product to process, with a corresponding shift in perceptions of students from their being learners (through teaching) to acquirers (through discovery) of language. Krashen has been a major influence, hypothesizing (1982) that with enough concentration on communication, grammar will take care of itself (i.e., will be acquired in natural order by an assimilation of linguistic data processed from comprehensible input). Consequently, language teachers have been looking more to sources of language in the environment and less to materials specially prepared for language learners.

Going on the assumption that learners might themselves learn language better than teachers can teach it, increasingly educators have put emphasis on the process of learning (as in the approach to writing described in Ch. 5), with suggestions that practice can best be generated by providing numerous activities involving real communication and a rich source of language data. The result has been a move towards learner-centered educational environments where the teacher becomes more a facilitator than a purveyor of knowledge disseminated from the head of the class. Thus language learning is thought to best be accomplished when language learning environments are non-threatening situations which make students feel at ease while giving them a responsible role in their own learning. Toward this end, teachers have been attempting to enlist students themselves as resources and informants, forming them into groups, getting them to speak to each other, write for each other, and to interact with each other in selecting options and responding to realistic challenges.

It would not be far-fetched to assume that a language teacher agreeing to many of the above statements might happen to observe a group of students who seemed to be enjoying a particular activity on the computer which was clearly not drill-and-practice. The question that should be forming in the teacher's mind is this: What is it about this activity that makes it so appealing, and how can I incorporate those factors into my own software development and/or utilization so that students will *want* to use the software to facilitate their own learning of a target language? I am about to suggest an answer hinging on three broad principles regarding the selection and production of humanistic CALL courseware: the principles of **intrinsic motivation**, **interactivity**, and **eclecticism**. Aspects of these three principles are represented schematically in Figure 1.

Intrinsic Motivation

- relevant and risk-free learning environment
- learning incidental to some other activity
- opportunities to use language in problem-solving
- multi-modal materials

Interactivity

- adjustment according to profile of individual student
- creation of environment facilitating interaction with computer
- creation of environment facilitating interaction with humans

Eclecticism

- creative adaptation of software designed for other audiences and purposes to classroom use in language learning

Figure 1. Principles for the Production and Selection of Humanistic Software

2.4　The Software Should Be Intrinsically Motivating

According to Moore and Anderson (1969), many cultures have evolved ways to impart learning through the use of games which are intrinsically motivating and relatively free of consequences, yet which are taken seriously by participants. Papert mentions two such activities in his book, *Mindstorms* (1980b, pp. 178–179): learning to hunt by "playful imitation," and learning Carnival dances at socially oriented Brazilian "samba schools." Papert aimed to create similarly motivating, yet risk-free, learning environments on computers. He called such environments, which students were encouraged to explore in order to discover how to function there, **microworlds**. Borrowing artificial intelligence techniques from Winograd's SHRDLU (1972), Higgins (1983) was among the first to apply this concept directly to language learning in his program GRAMMARLAND (see Ch. 1, "Lan-

guage"), which endowed the computer with a mini-language and an
ability to operate within that language (though the microworld concept was already inherent in a variety of simulation and adventure
games).

Stevick (1982) has noted the superiority of "the quality of learning that is incidental to something else we are trying to do" over that
which "takes place when we focus our attention only on the items
to be learned" (pp. 131–132). It is in thus subtly distracting the
learner that computers are especially effective. In microworld mode,
the computer is being used to provide game-like opportunities to use
language and to act in conjunction with that language. How those
opportunities are exploited, whether on the spot or in some consolidation activity later, depends, as with other media, largely on the
imagination of the teacher. Before reaching the point where they
must step back and take account of what they have assimilated, students are afforded the opportunity to enjoy language in a pleasant
and non-threatening way, and that enjoyment may even carry over
into the more thought-provoking consolidation later.

One singularly motivating aspect of computers exploited by microworlds is the challenge of figuring them out. Computers are impec-
cably logical, and the inherent logic in a problem or task can often be
elucidated from available data. Thus computers can present puzzles
which students, alone or in groups, can work to solve, taking into
account the available information and filtering this data through the
computer and/or one another to arrive at the rule governing the computer's behavior. Often, rules arrived at in this way can be tested,
and hypotheses confirmed or rejected, according to whether the computer responds in ways predicted by the induced rules. Put to such
use, computers become tools for discovery, and what is discovered
can be something about the language being studied.

Another motivating quality of computers is their ability to incorporate and accommodate other media. For example, graphics
and animation, used creatively but in moderation, can enhance ex-
plication and retention. Furthermore, computers interfaced with
videodiscs, voice digitizers, audio or video cassettes, or other audiovisual media, can compound the educational potential of these media
(see Ch. 1, "Inputting and Outputting Sounds and Video Images,"
for more detail). As Rubin (1984) puts it, "multi-modal materials
tend to attract and hold student's attention to a greater degree [with]

enormous implications for increasing learning" (p. 33).

Used in a "subtly distracting" way, as learning tools and facilitators (as what Marty, 1981, called "allies," and Higgins, 1983, called "pedagogue"), rather than as excuses for exercise books (Higgins' "magister"), and appropriately interfaced and programmed, computers can be compelling. Computers are indeed compelling when they satisfy human needs or desires such as the desire for novelty and challenge. Other needs of language learners which computers can help to satisfy are the needs for responsibility, options, and opportunities for communicative interaction. All of these features are likely to make courseware more intrinsically motivating to language learners.

2.5   The Software Should Be Truly Interactive

Interaction with a computer can be either unobtrusive or overt, the former taking place without the student's knowledge, whereas the latter simulates communication. Although truly viable (some would say plausible) communication is not presently available with computers themselves, computers do facilitate interaction with other communicative humans (see Chs. 1 and 6 for further discussion), and this latter attribute is taken by many to constitute their greatest potential in language learning.

Interaction with a Computer Can Be Unobtrusive

Interactivity has commonly been a feature of CALL programming. Typically this has meant that the program branches according to its author's anticipation of a certain student response. However, the fact that branching features can achieve greater sophistication than this type of anticipatory function has been supported by recent research on individual differences in students (as treated more fully in Ch. 3), a decidedly humanistic development.

In one such study, Chapelle and Jamieson (1986) report that, although students who had been tested to have a certain learning style disliked CALL on PLATO, one factor may have been the approach to CALL taken in the lessons themselves, which, like most CALL, was "notoriously 'insensitive' to individual learner differences" (p. 41). It follows that we may be doing some students an injustice by making them all work through the same lessons. Accordingly, computer programs could determine a student's learning style and then deliver a lesson appropriate for that student. Coupled with other media, options for individualization multiply. Rubin (1984, pp. 31–32) calls the videodisc a "superb vehicle" for developing learner profiles and then tracking students, "depending upon the student's learning style, language level or modality preference."

In another project considering individual differences in courseware development, Dalgish (1985) conducted error analysis studies on students of various languages and then produced generative CALL lessons which individualize tasks according to the student's first language. Still another consideration of individual differences in courseware design is pointed out by Johnson (1985), who cites evidence that girls may prefer cooperation in learning math while boys prefer competition. Clearly, the field would benefit from other studies isolating further areas where CALL can be individualized.

Providing Overt Interaction with Computers

Providing options within a lesson is crucial to viable CALL. Moore and Anderson (1969), in their discussion of clarifying educational environments, emphasize the importance of learners' being able to shift at will between several perspectives on learning, an idea that was to an extent validated for CALL by Stevens (1984). Given the existence of numerous options, computers can provide the ultimate in open-access, individualized instruction. Options can include instantaneous access to HELP panels, hints, and perhaps even solutions.

Because computers can frustrate by appearing obtuse, by failing to respond to what seems logical to the learner but was unanticipated by the programmer, there should be uncomplicated ways of moving around in the program. Whether to review a past section, advance to another, skip a frustrating problem, or simply to preview the material, where to go in the program and how to use it once there should be up to the user. Furthermore, there should always be a convenient total escape from a program. The best means of escape would provide an option to save the current state of the program, so that the learner could return to that point if desired. This is not always practical on personal computers, but at the very least, no program should make a learner feel that it is necessary to resort to switching off the system.

Feedback and other transactions with students can be presented randomly from a data base. This can be made to appear communicative, as in Johns' (1981) suggestion to store response components in chunks, presenting fewer chunks on subsequent passes through the program. In this way, the computer appears to become more familiar with the student, as would happen in normal conversation. For example, it might ask at first "Would you like to try again?" or "Do you care to have another go?", reducing (and interlacing) these responses on subsequent passes through the program to "Like to have another go?", "Care to try again?", "Another go?", "Again?", and so on, but varying the language even more with the addition of other sentence parts stored in the program.

Indeed, the question of communication with a computer is one of the most intriguing in CALL. A classic test for artificial intelligence, known as the Turing Test, puts a person in conversation with two devices, one of which is driven by a computer and the other by another human. If it cannot be distinguished which device is operated by the computer, then the computer is said to have passed the Turing Test. Whether this is possible at all with CALL software is not certain, nor is it certain whether it is necessary (compare the perspective of Ch.1, "Natural Language and Artificial Intelligence"). There is a need to determine whether or not a rich matrix of comprehensible input is possible with computers, and to learn more about the effects of "computerese" on language acquisition.

Communication in CALL is more often talked about than implemented. However, some interactive video projects, notably Montevidisco (Gale, 1983), achieve a high degree of simulated communication, and Kramsch, Morgenstern and Murray (1985) report on a project involving advanced parsing techniques to negotiate with students in a number of appealing ways. Underwood's (1984) methodological base and thirteen premises for communicative CALL are well conceived and often cited, but many of his examples of communicative software (ELIZA, for example), while perhaps of value in language learning, would fare poorly on the Turing Test. Articles like Barrutia's (1985), in which expert systems and their potential for communicative CALL are discussed, provide ideas for the future, but little of substance for the present.

Given developments in parsing and artificial intelligence (e.g.,

Addams, 1985), the quality of communicative interaction with computers will continue to improve, and it is possible that the communicative software available now meets communicative needs adequately (and certainly better than these needs are met with other media). However, it may be in putting students in touch with each other and with native speakers that the potential of CALL is best realized today.

Interaction with Other Humans

One need that people have in common is a need to communicate. This need is essentially what language teaching is all about, and computers happen to be very good at facilitating communication (a function explored at greater length in Ch. 6). Johnson (1985), on surveying a number of people active in CALL throughout the United States, found that "computer activities can serve as a catalyst that brings students together to interact, negotiate meaning, and negotiate strategies related to the task at hand," and that "peer and small group work centered around a computer-based activity can be a powerful force in a second language development program" (p. V-5). In addition, she notes "positive social effects of instructional work centered around computers." That group work has a beneficial effect on second language learners has been substantiated by Long and Porter (1985).

Discovery learning necessitates use of the language to communicate the discovery, thus creating situations ideal for socialization. Small groups often form spontaneously around a computer, and they can be convened more formally for deeper discussion of a problem or simulation. In such cases, students will have more than an artificial need to communicate; they will have real information to share, and may even be spurred to improve their reading and communicative skills in English specifically to be able to cope with and impart information related to such activities (as evidenced in Taylor, 1986a).

The most universally used communications software is word processing software (see Ch. 5, this volume; also Daiute, 1983, for an excellent characterization of how word processing facilitates writing). Such communication is facilitated by the fact that for many users, writing on a computer is itself intrinsically motivating. Marcus (1983) has coined the term *videotext* to describe text that, in flitting about the screen, takes on many of the appealing qualities of video. Videotext may be a factor in motivating writing within the context of a composition assignment, and when used communicatively, videotext facilitates collaborative efforts. Marcus suggests, for example, that students exchange computer screens so that one can comment on the other's writing while it is in progress. Daiute (1985) suggests other forms of collaborative writing, particularly of plays, and in use of the computer as a dynamic blackboard for group revision. Collaborative uses are also described by Friel (1985), who stresses that, when exploiting courseware in language learning, one must consider that "what at first seem autonomous exercises may, if successful, be combined to form parts of a more complex classroom exercise" (p. 37).

Other configurations may place students in direct communication through satellite or telephone links; PLATO, for example, allows conferencing across oceans, and Crookal (cited in Dunkel, 1986) has had students engage in internationally played simulations. Other forms of computer-based communication, such as electronic mail and bulletin boards, tend to elicit spontaneous communication even from non-native speakers. Alternatively, the text and graphics capabilities of computers can be combined in appealing ways (see Ch. 4 for discussion in relation to reading software), encouraging students to produce greeting cards, newspapers, yearbooks, and other more or less ambitious documents of which they can be proud.

2.6 Eclecticism: Going Beyond CALL Software

Much has been written to the effect that there is little available in the way of CALL software, or that what is available is disappointing. This may be true, strictly speaking, in that software made specifically for an audience of language learners is frequently found lacking. But if one is looking for authentic text meted out in manageable quantities and used in situations which appear natural, then the criterion for "language learning software" broadens.

Often, educational software designed for native speakers has an editor with which lexis can be changed, and there is much courseware which, though not designed specifically for education, is rich in language that foreign or second language learners will be motivated to learn in order to participate in an activity or in the discussion that might follow a session with the software. Baltra (1984), for example, has documented successful communication and learning in a language class based on a commercial adventure game that engages students and teachers as equal collaborators in trying to find the solution to a mystery. Similarly, Taylor (1986b) relates experiences with a "sophisticated" commercial simulation game in which "much of the vocabulary is new, but students have little difficulty learning it" (p. 12). Similarly, public domain software, while lacking in some production features of its commercial counterpart, often comprises unique and entertaining programs useful to language learning. Since there is usually free access to the source code, public domain programs are infinitely more adaptable to one's own language learning or teaching situation (for suggestions, see Stevens, 1985 and 1986).

Software that offers training in problem-solving and higher-order thinking skills is of particular interest from a humanistic point of view because it lends itself to collaborative work by the students, who must manipulate the program—e.g., by creating some kind of simple machine or figure—to achieve a certain goal. Pogrow (cited in Johnson, 1985) found that limited English-proficient students who used such software had 50% more friends than those in a control group, possibly because of increased opportunities to interact with peers and native speakers, and increased confidence in their cognitive competence.

Johnson (1985) concluded from her survey that "the use of a computer as a tool to accomplish functional tasks has far greater potential for second language learning than traditional or even communicative CALL" (p. III-5). She suggests that the study of language *per se* on computers be "a by-product when focusing on tasks related to both social and academic success in school" (p. III-6). Thus one might employ science lab or economics simulations as CALL courseware. Another excellent but often overlooked exploitation of functional software in language learning is programming languages, and there is at least one textbook (Abdulaziz, Smalzer, and Abdulaziz, 1985) for teaching language through the medium of programming. Similarly, skills such as typing, word processing, use of writing aids, and spreadsheet and database manipulation, can be taught as part of what is really a language course (see Barlow, 1987).

2.7 Conclusion

There are numerous features of computers that are uniquely exploitable in language learning, many of which were not utilized in behaviorist-based courseware but which have begun to appear as CALL development has adapted to current trends in language teaching methodology. Current uses have placed the computer in such roles as linguistic informant, game partner, a means of getting a message out to a variety of people, a tool, or even a drill master if that is what students want. And some do. Before entirely abandoning drill-and-practice software, teachers should give it a try with a foreign language they themselves want to learn. They can then form their own assessment of the efficacy of drill-and-practice, based on insights gleaned from a learner's perspective.

Language teachers who have applied the principles of intrinsic motivation, interactivity, and eclecticism in their selection and development of CALL courseware have begun to see that computers, used in a variety of ways, can attend to individual differences among learners and take on roles supportive of humanistic language learning. Adherence to these principles, and discovery of new ones through research and classroom practice, will constantly improve the ability of computers to facilitate the language learning process.

Research

3 Research Trends in Computer-Assisted Language Learning

Carol Chapelle
and
Joan Jamieson

3.1 Introduction

Because computer use in instruction is at a relatively early stage of development, evaluation of computer-assisted language learning (CALL) necessarily includes general and observable features such as whether the programs work, the screen displays are pleasing, adequate instructions are given, and answers are judged appropriately. Initially, teachers are told to look for these features in reviewing CALL materials, but eventually CALL must be examined with an eye toward the curriculum of a particular language program and the learners for whom it is intended.

The evolving pedagogical framework for assessing CALL which was outlined in the preceding chapter is elaborated here through a summary of research findings and trends. This review of research directions in computer-assisted language learning summarizes the methods, findings, and problems of the exploration of CALL effectiveness. It begins by isolating salient questions related to CALL use. On this basis, a review is presented of effectiveness studies that examine differences between CALL and conventional instruction, effects of various CALL lesson strategies, and the relationships between lesson approaches and learner characteristics. Research on attitudes and interaction patterns is described. Answers provided by research to questions about CALL lead into considerations for future research.

3.2   The Question of CALL Effectiveness

Limited by time and space, any CALL lesson uses specific approaches
to focus on only certain aspects of language learning. Examination
of a single lesson will rarely reveal that it is good for every purpose
or every student. Instead, a given lesson on a particular topic will be
suitable for some students. Thus, the question "Is CALL effective?"
leads to many more questions than answers:

- Do students who use CALL learn more efficiently than those
  who do not?

- Are there particular lesson strategies that are better in general?

- Are there some lesson strategies that are better for particular
  learners?

- Do students like to use CALL?

- What kind of learning takes place while students are using
  CALL?

To address these issues, courseware is sometimes tested on
students to see whether it is effective in teaching the material. Unfortunately, the methods typically used to evaluate CALL effectiveness
produce answers that can be difficult to interpret. Problems with
evaluations of language courseware stem from attempts to match
two things that are not well understood: second language acquisition and courseware use. Because the process of second language
acquisition is not completely understood, it is difficult to make direct recommendations for evaluating learning tasks on- or off-line.
Similarly, the unique characteristics of a particular computer lesson
are difficult to define. If lessons are to be evaluated in light of what
is known about second language acquisition, questions about students' development resulting from use of particular lessons need to
be answered.

3.3 Research on CALL as a Predictor of Achievement

Control-Treatment Designs

When computers were introduced into education in the early 1960's, researchers naturally wanted to evaluate this new, expensive, but potentially useful medium. Numerous studies across disciplines were carried out to attempt to discover whether computer-using students learned better and faster than students taught by traditional methods. The typical research design provided CALL materials for an experimental group and traditional instruction for a control group.

These computer-assisted instruction (CAI) studies have yielded primarily positive, and some neutral, results over the past twenty-five years. Studies in which CALL-using students did better than a control group receiving conventional instruction include two studies of students learning basic language skills (Buckley and Rauch, 1979; Sarracho, 1982). Another, in which CALL was used to teach grammar in a journalism class, found that the CALL-using group made greater gains in their post-test scores over their pre-test scores (Oates, 1981). Russian translation was taught more effectively through the use of a CALL program (Van Campen, 1981). Also, one group of ESL students improved their punctuation use with a CALL program (Freed, 1971), and another group made progress in writing using a text analysis program (Reid, 1986).

In contrast to these positive results, CALL drill-and-practice lessons did not effect any greater achievement than ordinary instruction in a written French course (Brebner, Johnson, and Mydlarski, 1984). An experimental group of students in grades 3 to 7 using a reading program ten minutes daily made no greater reading gains than the students in the non-CALL sections (Lysiak, Wallace, and Evans, 1976). There were no differences in writing outcomes between students who had used a composition feedback program and those who had not (Anandam, Kotler, Eisel, and Roche, 1979) and no significant differences were found between control and CALL treatment groups in community college English classes (Murphy and Appel, 1977).

Neither studies of CALL nor those of CAI have provided unequivocal evidence for the superiority of computerized over conventional instruction. However, these results have prompted greater scrutiny of the methods used to assess effectiveness. Problems have been pointed out with specific studies such as one in which CAI and lecture discussion sections of the same courses (composition and algebra) were compared. A significant, positive impact on achievement was reported; however, dramatic decreases in course completion rates in the CAI groups allow for the possibility that only good students had remained in that course (Alderman, 1978).

A more universal problem with studies of this type is that "the nature of the learning tasks, the characteristics of the learners, and the characteristics of the media [are] largely ignored" when the research is designed and interpreted (Jonassen, 1985, p. 30). Without an understanding of specific attributes of the situation, it is difficult to know what learning effects ought to be attributed to (Clark, 1985).

Comparisons of Lesson Strategies

Criticisms of this research have resulted in a recasting of the question of CALL effectiveness to a more careful analysis of specific features of the medium that may be conducive to learning. Some studies have isolated features such as the kind of language used in a lesson as a basis for examining the effects of a particular aspect of a lesson.

Schaeffer (1981) compared the effects of using "meaningful" versus structural German lessons. Although by current standards the definition of "meaningful" was restricted, findings indicated that students who used lessons in which they had to understand the meaning of the language to answer correctly did better on both meaningful and structural post-tests than did students who practiced with lessons in which exercises could be done mechanically—without processing meaning. Another lesson strategy comparison, which assessed retention of German from video with varying degrees of interactivity, found that the interactive video condition was the one in which the subjects remembered the material best (Schrupp, Busch, and Mueller, 1983). A third study, which compared the difference in effects of different sequences of presentation for German vocabulary items, found some sequences superior to others for long term retention (Beard, Bar, Fletcher, and Atkinson, 1975).

A more thorough study testing the effects of lesson strategies isolated six pedagogical and four answer-judging principles established on the basis of research in cognitive psychology and second language acquisition (Robinson, 1986). Using this foundation, experimental lessons were developed and compared to typical lessons that did not reflect such principles. For example, the hypothesis that use of a context for "introduction of discrete structural items will improve memory and subsequent learning of the items" (p. 17) was tested by providing an experimental group with a contextualized grammar lesson and a control group with a lesson containing semantically unrelated items. Although the results for each hypothesis tested did not always favor the experimental group for short-term learning, the overall conclusion was that there was a "high level of confidence that instructional treatments did significantly favor the experimental group" (p. 35) on the post-test, which required retention of material over the course of the semester (for discussion, see Doughty, 1986, and Pennington, 1986a).

This kind of research provides an important first step toward empirical support for principles from theory and research which can offer general suggestions for courseware development such as those that have been summarized by Jay (1983). For individualized instruction, however, more learner-specific suggestions are needed.

Lesson Approaches and Learners

For the study of CALL effectiveness, as in the examination of the effects of various language teaching methods, assessment of the interaction between learner characteristics and effectiveness of approach are needed. A few studies have attempted to choose appropriate materials for students on the basis of their cognitive styles.

One study examined the interaction between lesson type and one **cognitive style**, i.e., **field-independence**—the ability to attend to relevant information without being distracted by the surroundings (Abraham, 1985). Students were given one of two different types of lessons on forming participial phrases. One used a rule presentation (deductive) approach and the other presented examples of the structure (inductive). Field-independent students learned better with the deductive lesson, while the field-dependent students learned better with the inductive lesson. A comparison of the means from the post-test scores revealed no significant differences in performance on the basis of the type of lesson alone, so that if cognitive style had not been considered in this comparison of lesson types, it would have appeared that there was no difference in terms effectiveness of the two lesson strategies.

A study which assessed students' **reflection/impulsivity** found that impulsive students performed better on an oral sentence construction task in Spanish when the program forced them to wait before responding. This "stop and think" strategy that the program made them use improved their performance on the task (Meredith, 1978). In another study, students' conceptual level was significantly predictive of their preference and need for structure in their second language learning environment (Zampogna, Gentile, Papalia, and Silber, 1976).

This research points toward the need to examine student characteristics such as cognitive style in concert with effectiveness of particular lesson approaches. However, cognitive styles are difficult to assess and their relationships to instruction types are not well understood. Should there be an attempt to match lesson types to cognitive style, or should the attempt be to teach strategies to students whose cognitive style is typically unsuccessful in certain language acquisition environments? As a way to gain insight into these questions, some researchers have turned to a closer examination of the learning process.

Research on the Relationship between CALL and Student Attitudes

A second aspect of CALL research has addressed the well-established importance of attitudes in second language acquisition by asking the question: Do students like to use CALL?

Observations of students' CALL attitudes have been made both informally and through use of attitude questionnaires. For example, Dixon (1981, p. 105) reported that ESL students were "happy" and usage was "high so something must be right" with the ESL CALL lessons on the PLATO system at the University of Illinois. Reid, Lindstrom, McCaffrey, and Larson (1983, p.41) reported that all of the ESL students who used a text analysis program for composition "enjoyed the cultural experience." Questionnaire results typically—but not always—indicate favorable attitudes toward CALL. For example, positive attitudes were found in the studies of CALL for written French (Brebner, Johnson, and Mydlarski, 1984), English grammar (Oates, 1981), and reading (Lysiak, Wallace, and Evans, 1976). However, poor attitudes for CALL were reported by Alderman (1978), and Sarracho (1982) found that the students who did not use CALL had better attitudes toward it than those who did.

Although these observations indicate something about overall attitudes, they share the problems of studies of effectiveness: They attempt to summarize the attitudes of all students to the use of CALL in general. A more useful direction would be to note attitudes toward specific features of programs. For example, Robinson (1986) reported that students demonstrated positive attitudes toward some features of the experimental lessons employed in the study. Analysis of these features reveal principles of design that may stimulate positive attitudes.

Stable learner characteristics may also have an impact on students' attitudes toward CALL materials. In a study of ESL students using CALL, field-independent students tended to have a negative attitude toward the lessons, while field-dependent students tended to like them (Chapelle and Jamieson, 1986). The study by Sarracho (1982) that found negative attitudes of users toward CALL suggested that results might be accounted for by ethnic differences in learning styles. Another relevant study (teaching programming) in which ability level was found to be a significant negative predictor of attitude toward the lessons, concluded that "students with high scores did not feel challenged and therefore developed an unfavorable attitude" (Rushinek, Rushinek, and Stutz, 1985, p. 261).

To adequately assess attitude toward CALL, both lesson and learner variables must be examined. If students believe lessons are appropriate and useful, they are likely to have a good attitude toward them. Appropriateness appears to be a function of characteristics such as cognitive style and ability level.

3.4   Learning Processes and CALL Research

Given the complexity of lesson and learner variables, some researchers have begun to examine learning processes by observing interaction patterns of students as they work on computer materials. In some studies, amount of time spent by the learner in interaction with the computer is examined in relation to other variables. For example, when Curtin, Avner, and Provenzano (1981) investigated students' error rate, rate of interaction, total time, and review time on computerized Russian lessons, they found some relationships of these processes to the content material being used, and to the subsequent success of the students in the course.

The computer was also used to collect data in a study of ESL students' learning strategies, such as monitoring. These have been found be related to cognitive style, such as field-independence (Jamieson, 1986). A similar approach was taken in a study of writing strategies employed by writers using a word processor. Key strokes were collected and plotted to reveal the patterns of pausing, revising, and rereading that comprise the writer's "composing rhythm" (O'Meara, 1986). Another study of writing strategies used videotape to detail the processes that writers engage in on- and off-line (Wahlstrom, 1986).

Types of interaction among students initiated by use of computer materials has also been investigated. For example, a study describing differences in learning processes of students working on activities on- and off-line revealed some minor differences in the students' turn-taking behavior and differences in the kinds of reading strategies employed in the two contexts (Windeatt, 1986). Another study examined the number and kinds of functions of spoken language used by pairs of ESL students as they worked on three different types of programs: (1) ELIZA (see Ch. 1, "Natural Language and Artificial Intelligence," for description), (2) a commercially successful simulation involving problem-solving, and (3) a traditional grammar drill on definite and indefinite articles (Liou, 1986). The analysis revealed that, for the three pairs of students, the simulation program "elicited the most talk and provided the most practice of language functions" (p. 45). The drill on articles "prompted consideration and discussion of language forms, [and] elicited the largest variety of functions" (p. 46). On the basis of this analysis, ELIZA elicited the least language.

The study of learning processes in CALL presents a difficult problem of data analysis and interpretation. Nevertheless, the analysis of data in these studies may help to clarify some of the questions about learning processes that have arisen in the simpler research designs. The study of learning processes which is now taking place in second language acquisition research (Cohen and Hosenfeld, 1981), writing research (Swarts, Flower, and Hayes, 1983), and psychology (Ericsson and Simon, 1984) may shed light on some of the learning outcomes that have been observed in studies of CALL achievement and attitude. For example, in a study of children's acquisition of advertising concepts through the use of a computer lesson, the data collected by the program allowed the researchers to observe that field-dependent learners tended to use the optional examples more than their field-independent counterparts (Carrier, Davidson, Higson, and Williams, 1984). This kind of learning process, which was related in that study to a field-dependent cognitive style, must be examined in relation to success on particular tasks.

The research studies summarized in this section are presented in outline form in Figure 1.

3.5   Prospects for CALL Research

Answers to Questions

These studies on CALL (summarized in Figure 1) provide only tentative answers to the questions of CALL effectiveness. They do, however, point clearly to directions for future research.

Do students who use CALL learn more efficiently than those who do not? This question is too simple to answer directly. Both CALL materials and language learners differ from one another in ways that affect learning. It is not useful to talk about CAI materials as though they all encompassed one homogeneous approach to language learning. Nor is it accurate to think of learners as all of one type. Future research which approaches this question must include an assessment of the characteristics of learners and materials.

Are there some lesson strategies that are better, in general, than others? Some empirical evidence supports the possibility that lesson strategies reflecting principles of cognitive psychology—particularly with respect to the importance of meaningful learning—are most effective. However, the assessment of many aspects of lesson design may need to be considered in light of the learners for whom the lessons are intended.

Are there some lesson strategies which are better for particular learners? This question of appropriate lessons for individual learners is a particularly interesting one for development of individualized instruction. Research in this area is quite new and it suffers from a poor understanding of the measurement and effects of individual learning styles. However, by exploring learning processes and testing hypotheses, insights can be gained into the crucial variables that

ACHIEVEMENT	ATTITUDES	LEARNING PROCESSES
CAI vs. Traditional Instruction Alderman (1978) Anandam et al. (1979)	Brebner et al. (1984) Chapelle and Jamieson (1986)	Carrier et al. (1984) Curtin et al. (1981)
Beard et al. (1975) Brebner et al. (1984) Buckley and Rauch (1979) Freed (1971) Lysiak et al. (1976) Murphy and Appel (1977) Oates (1981) Reid (1986) Sarracho (1982) Van Campen (1981)	Dixon (1981) Lysiak et al. (1976) Oates (1981) Reid et al. (1983) Robinson (1986) Rushinek et al. (1985) Sarracho (1982)	Jamieson (1986) Liou (1986) O'Meara (1986) Wahlstrom (1986) Windeatt (1986)
Different Lesson Approaches Beard et al. (1975) Robinson (1986) Schaeffer (1981) Schrupp et al. (1983)		
Lesson Approaches and Learners Abraham (1985) Merideth (1978) Zampogna et al. (1976)		

Figure 1. Summary of Research Related to Aspects of CALL Effectiveness

comprise the process of individualized instruction.

Do students like to use CALL? Numerous studies have reported overall positive attitudes towards CALL use; however, when other student characteristics were examined in conjunction with CALL attitudes, it was revealed that some students like to use some kinds of CALL while others do not. Students tend to like to use CALL if the materials are meaningful and appropriate for them.

What kind of learning takes place while students are using CALL? Research on this question is just commencing. Through the use of techniques such as videotaping and the collecting of on-line data on students as they work, more can be learned about the processes involved in various types of computerized learning as compared to off-line activities. What is discovered about learning processes may shed light on the variety of results attained in studies of learning outcomes, or products.

Questions to Be Answered

The research methodologies and results that have been reviewed point to aspects of lessons, learning, and learners that must be more clearly defined to make a meaningful assessment of CALL effectiveness. One useful approach for defining salient aspects of computer lessons is presented by Phillips (1986, pp. 26–27), who suggests a seven-faceted analysis of CALL materials. Phillips defines **activity type** as the type of exercise—e.g., game, quiz, drill. Related, but not equivalent, to activity type is **learning type**, the emphasis of student learning on either specific points or more generalized language processing strategies. The **learner focus** is what the student is consciously working on while interacting with the lesson. This is sometimes distinct from the **program focus**, which refers to the linguistic purpose of the activity. **Language difficulty** is the level of language used in the program, and the **program difficulty** refers to how tolerant of the learner's performance the program is. **Classroom management** is the way the program is used and integrated into the rest of the classroom environment. Lessons employed in research studies of CALL effectiveness can be defined along these dimensions to help clarify research results.

The learning strategies employed by users of particular lessons need to be described. Strategies studied have included on-line interaction patterns of individual students as they work on lessons, and

computer stimulated off-line interaction among learners. Evidence
for a number of strategies has been identified; however, this kind of
research is as exploratory with on-line materials as it is with other
materials, so that it is necessary to continue to search for and define
strategies.

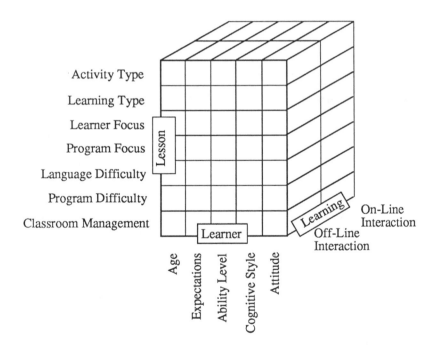

Figure 2. Dimensions of Analysis for Lessons, Learners and Learning

Five student characteristics are important for assessing CALL
effectiveness. First, appropriate courseware may be different for
learners of **different ages**. While children have the time and the
inclination to learn through exploration and play, as Papert (1980b)

suggests, adults typically have less time and a greater ability to pursue specific objectives. Second, **expectations based on prior learning experiences** might partially determine the kinds of materials that will be effective for particular learners. Third, **ability level** may impact effectiveness because, for example, good learners may not need or want the specific program guidance that unsuccessful learners need (Steinberg, 1977). Fourth, **cognitive style** such as field-independence/dependence and reflection/impulsivity need to be assessed in the use and effectiveness of CALL. Fifth, **the dynamic relationship between attitude and CALL variables** needs to be examined. The relationships between the three dimensions of analysis—**lesson, learning,** and **learner**—are represented in the three-dimensional model shown in Figure 2.

3.6 Conclusion

Bringing lesson, learning, and learner variables into the CALL effectiveness question may seem overwhelming to some. It would be much easier to simply study, in the behaviorist tradition (as outlined in Ch. 2), the effects of all CALL treatments on the behavior of subjects. However, to gain an understanding of how particular CALL materials can be used most effectively in the complex second language acquisition process, it is necessary to ask difficult questions—questions about lesson features, learning processes, and learner characteristics.

Currently, computer-assisted learning materials "are limited by their lack of general knowledge about the learning topic, about the student and about the teaching/learning process" (Hartley, 1985, p. 140). In many cases, they are necessarily limited; CALL materials cannot be based on insights about second language acquisition until those insights become available. The effective use of CALL requires an understanding of how learners might best learn; therefore, researchers must continue to study the effects of variables on second language acquisition in a range of learning environments, including CALL.

Reading

4 Computers and Reading Skills: The Medium and the Message

David H. Wyatt

4.1 Introduction

This chapter on computers and reading skills is part of a state of the art survey of computer applications in second and foreign language learning. As such, it faces a host of theoretical and practical questions, ranging from current disagreements on approaches for language pedagogy to rapid advances in computer hardware, as described in earlier chapters of this volume. Some of these topics will be addressed in later sections. The primary aim of the chapter, however, is to bring into sharper focus the nature and pedagogical capabilities of the computer as a new medium for the teaching and learning of reading.

4.2 The Computer—A "New" Medium?

Mainframe and minicomputer systems have been used in computer-assisted language learning (CALL) for over two decades. Recently, the advent of inexpensive microcomputer hardware has made the computer a familiar presence in the classroom, workshop, and conference session. However, the apparent familiarity of computers in second and foreign language learning is deceptive. In many important respects, the computer remains a new medium.

The types of computer applications currently representative of CALL show all the characteristics of a medium in its infancy. When a new medium is introduced, there is a natural tendency to begin using it in ways that directly parallel applications in more familiar media. It may be a considerable time before the real potential and unique characteristics of the new medium start to exert their effect on theories and techniques developed for the older media. While the possibilities may be revolutionary, the process of harnessing the power of the new medium is often a slow, evolutionary one.

4.3   Computer Capabilities and Reading

In terms of current or rapidly-developing hardware and software capabilities, it is clearly feasible for computers to play an extensive role in the development of reading skills. At the low end, the computer medium can be used to introduce and develop recognition skills with a new alphabet. At higher levels, computers can provide an extensive range of mechanical and meaningful reading exercises, and can assist in the development and checking of discourse-level comprehension abilities.

In terms of raw potential, the computer medium is well matched to the requirements of reading activities. However, almost none of the existing CALL courseware for second and foreign language reading skills has moved beyond the stage of directly paralleling the activities found in printed textbooks. This is no reason for rejecting such software; each program should be judged on its own merits.

For the purposes of discussion, three types of CALL reading activities can be identified: those which are **direct parallels of familiar paradigms** in print or other media; those which represent **interesting extensions of familiar activities**; and those which embody **significant new possibilities** in the computer medium. The discussion of the first type of software would provide little basis for evaluating the potential of the computer. Therefore, rather than addressing the first CALL category and limiting this paper to a review of current courseware, the next two sections will present idealized descriptions of some interesting **evolutionary** and **revolutionary** applications of the computer medium in reading.

4.4 Significant CALL Extensions of Familiar Reading Activities

Reading Laboratories

One common principle in some approaches to the development of reading skills is to provide students with reading materials at a level slightly above their current reading proficiency so as to provide a challenge without causing counterproductive frustration. A second principle is to provide a selection of reading materials so that students can choose topics of genuine interest. A third is to permit each student to complete the reading and any activities based on it at a comfortable individual pace.

Clearly, it is difficult to provide this type of individualized reading through the medium of the textbook or reader. This has led to the development of integrated sets of reading materials often referred to as **reading laboratories**. Such labs include sets of reading passages on different topics—with comprehension-checking and other activities—at each of several reading proficiency levels. Students read passages at their own pace, complete practice activities, and check their work against answer keys.

Computer-based reading laboratories can continue the evolutionary movement away from the printed textbook for this component of the reading class. Although parallel to the printed card labs, the CALL versions are of interest because of their greatly enhanced capabilities. Computer-based labs can offer an enormously expanded range of topics at more finely-graded proficiency levels. Where appropriate, each reading passage can be made available in a large number of versions along a continuum from the authentic original prose to a greatly simplified beginning-level version. Thus, a student encountering real difficulties after starting to read a passage in its original form is able to step down to a simplified version.

If desired, voice tracks can provide an audio presentation of each version of the reading. This would be a high fidelity digitized human voice, not synthesized speech (for comparison of digitized and synthesized speech, see Ch. 1, "Inputting and Outputting Sound and Video Images"). If appropriate, graphics, animation, and motion pictures can accompany the reading. Activities based on the passage—comprehension, vocabulary, and the like—will profit from the basic CALL advantages of interaction and individualization. Management of student work with the lab is simplified from both the teacher's and students' point of view. Individual students' problems with specific areas of vocabulary and comprehension can be considered when selecting practice activities to be presented with the next reading passage.

Two new developments in data storage technology (see Ch. 1 for overview), known as CD–ROM and CD–I, offer the basis for the claim of radically greater potential for computer-medium reading laboratories. **CD–ROM** (compact disc–read only memory) is closely related to laser videodisc and compact audiodisc technology, but is oriented principally towards text storage (Lambert and Ropiequet, 1986). CD–ROM discs and microcomputer-controlled players are already a reality. An interesting example is the 21-volume Grolier *Academic American Encyclopedia*; this is now available on a single CD–ROM disc costing less than the printed volumes.

CD–I (compact disc–interactive) takes this exciting concept to its logical conclusion by adding the storage of all types of computer text and data to the videodisc's sound and video capabilities. With CD–I, for example, high-fidelity sound, still graphics, animation, and even motion picture sequences can be made available to illustrate the text on an encyclopedia disc (Raleigh, 1986). It should be emphasized that no CD–I discs have yet been produced; the standard for CD–I data storage techniques was proposed as recently as March 1986 (Helliwell, 1986).

Despite their obvious educational applications, general-purpose CD–ROM and CD–I discs would not suffice to fully exploit the potential of a computer-based reading laboratory. Custom-produced discs would have to be created to provide different versions of a topic at a variety of reading proficiency levels, appropriate audio and graphic components, etc. Or rather, given the enormous storage capacity, a single CD–I disc can contain reading laboratories for English language arts (grades K–12), English as a second language, and all the commonly taught foreign languages. The development and testing of a CD–I reading lab disc would be an expensive proposition. The mass production costs would be small, however, and within the next two years CD–ROM players will begin to take their place as common, inexpensive storage devices.

In summary, the key contributions of the computer medium in reading lab applications are its enormous storage capacity and consequent ability to provide highly individualized reading materials. Computer-based reading labs would also share the more general CALL advantages of self-pacing and automated recordkeeping and management. Where desirable, fast, convenient access to a high-quality audio accompaniment can also be provided.

Higher-Level Reading Skills

An increasingly common component of reading courses at the intermediate level and beyond is a treatment of certain **higher-level reading skills** that become particularly important for full comprehension of discourse (Wyatt, 1984b). Some of these skills involve recognition of referential relationships. For example, stylistic considerations often prompt writers to avoid repetitive use of a single term; instead, two or more expressions may be used to vary the presentation, as with the terms *software*, *courseware*, and *programs* in this paper. Frequently, the terms are not exact synonyms, as with *software* and *courseware*. In well-written prose, the writer's intent that different terms be recognized as exactly synonymous is clear to a skilled reader. Less able readers, however, may need activities to help them develop this skill. Another example of referential relationships is the use of anaphora (backwards reference) and cataphora (forwards reference). Such references may span several sentences and present comprehension problems for less skilled readers, who may need assistance and practice in recognizing the referential meaning (Mackay, 1974).

A second type of high-level reading skill involves grasping the rhetorical structure of discourse (Selinker, Todd-Trimble and Trimble, 1978; Bensoussan, 1986). Rhetorical forms such as narrative, classification, process description, and extended definition may occupy single paragraphs, groups of paragraphs, or longer stretches of discourse. Skilled readers will, for example, readily identify the beginning and end of a multi-paragraph classification forming part of a chapter in a text, and this will assist them in mentally organizing, understanding, and remembering the information. Practice in recognizing key notional and functional cues (*may be divided into / classified as ...; the final type / class / kind / category of ...*) may help develop the global comprehension skills of the less proficient reader.

A final example of high-level reading skills is the use of schemata

(Carrell and Eisterhold, 1983). A fundamental aspect of the reading process is the constant activity of the reader in establishing expectancies and making predictions concerning what is to come, based upon the reading so far. In essence, a schema is a generalized set of expectations. For example, "I made the call from a small post office just outside Algiers" may evoke a number of schemata, or scripts, one of which might represent expectations of familiar post office surroundings, telephone equipment, and self-dialing procedures. A student of French might be far from anticipating the reality: waiting in line to tell a clerk the number to call, waiting for the clerk to place the call and tell you which numbered booth to enter, and lining up to pay the clerk after the call. If the narrative spelled all this out, the reader would probably be surprised but not confused. However, a more oblique narrative might cause serious comprehension problems for readers who lacked the cultural schema assumed by the writer. Practice with important culturally determined schemata and with readings that assume an awareness of them should help develop the reader's skill in grasping the full meaning of the discourse (Melendez and Pritchard, 1985).

Perhaps the greatest single obstacle to the presentation and practice of these and other discourse-level features in the print medium is the sheer volume of text that is needed. For example, a minimum treatment of classification might require five to ten complete reading passages, each including a single or multi-paragraph classification structure. This alone would occupy a large part of a normal-sized textbook. Of course, some of the passages might well be usable as illustrations of different rhetorical or other high-level discourse features. However, they would generally need to be reordered and interspersed with new passages for each different teaching purpose. While difficult in print, these operations are trivial in the computer medium, with its enormous storage capacity and great flexibility of retrieval and display.

Faster and More Efficient Reading

In courses to develop second and foreign language reading skills, direct attention is sometimes paid to the improvement of students' reading speed and efficiency (Fry, 1963; Hamp-Lyons, 1983). In part, this is in recognition of research evidence which reveals that skillful, efficient readers tend to take in larger groups of words with a single eye fixation and make fewer regressions to earlier parts of the passage. It is also due to experience with poor readers who, in approaching reading as a word-by-word decoding task, appear to find it much harder to recognize the higher levels of sentence, paragraph, and discourse meaning.

Two basic approaches have been used in the **faster and more efficient reading** components of reading courses. One is to provide frequent timed reading practice using printed passages simplified to the student's current ability level. With few problems of vocabulary or syntax to derail them, students should be able to concentrate on reading fluently for overall meaning. The computer can contribute to this approach in a number of ways, including finer matching of passages to individual ability level and automated management of this course component.

The second type of approach attempts to exercise more direct influence over the student's reading habits. One technique has involved dividing a reading into meaningful groups of words and presenting the groups in carefully timed succession to encourage students to read them with a single eye fixation. Although this can be simulated with a printed page, a filmstrip-like device called a **tachistoscope** has been the best method for implementing the approach.

For the second type of faster reading activity, the computer medium offers dramatic improvements over the best method previously available. The **dynamic video screen** offers virtually complete control over the speed and position of appearance of letters, words, phrases, and sentences in a reading passage. To a far greater extent than previously possible, this medium can influence how students perceive and read. Even the presentation typeface can readily be varied to provide different types of reading practice, including factors such as printed versus cursive forms, upper/lower case, and size. The overall speed of presentation and readability of the passage can be automatically adjusted based on a student's demonstrated level of comprehension.

It should be noted that research evidence on the efficacy of this second type of direct, analytic practice in faster reading is not decisive. It seems likely that the far greater power of computers to effectively implement faster reading techniques will offer opportunities for a much more conclusive assessment of the value of this type of intervention. Indeed, one of the more exciting avenues opened up by the computer medium will be the enhanced ability to test some aspects of the continuing conflict between integrative, natural approaches and analytic, practice-before-communication approaches (Brown, 1982). In these tests, the computer will function as a neutral data collector. As I have argued elsewhere (Wyatt, 1984c), the computer medium has no inherent bias towards either integrative or analytic approaches to language learning, despite attempts to characterize it as an analytic medium.

4.5   Reading Activities Made Possible by the Computer Medium

One of the principal themes of this paper is to emphasize the importance of recognizing that the computer essentially remains a new medium for language learning. To that end, a distinction has been drawn between CALL reading activities which are significant extensions of familiar paradigms in print or other media (**evolutionary** applications, covered in the previous section) and those that represent new possibilities (**revolutionary** CALL activities, to be discussed in this section). In reality, however, the two categories overlap. With the dramatically greater degree of control afforded by the computer in faster reading materials, for example, a case can be made for including such activities in this section on new possibilities. Conversely, many of the CALL examples in this section are related in some ways to familiar practices.

Annotation

In the print medium, annotation of reading passages is a common student aid. Its various forms have included numbered or italicized words and phrases with accompanying paraphrases or translations in margins or footnotes, other marginalia such as outline guides, and the like. Though doubtless helpful to readers, this fixed type of annotation represents an inelegant and intrusive superimposition of information that distracts from and reduces the authenticity of the reading experience.

Computers make possible a striking transformation of this venerable idea. The two key elements are **transparency** and **learner control**. It is the dynamic computer screen that provides the key to transparent annotation in this medium. A very wide range of learner aids can be provided to accompany each reading passage—as comprehensive as desired. These might include notes on vocabulary, syntax, function, cultural values, discourse structure, plot, characterization, stylistics, and more.

In the basic mode of presentation, the reading passage would appear in authentic, undisturbed fashion on the computer screen. However, the extensive layers of help would be instantly available to the reader at the touch of one or two computer keys. Point and click with a mouse control, and a temporary screen window opens, perhaps displaying vocabulary help. Touch a different key and a tall, narrow window opens to show a diagram of the rhetorical structure of the paragraph. Point to and click on an unclear reference and the referent is temporarily highlighted. When any of this help is no longer needed, a single keypress can remove everything except the passage, restoring the screen to its original condition. The annotation is thus completely transparent—its functioning is invisible to the user, except when called upon.

The second element, learner control, is implicit in the discussion in the previous paragraph. In the approach to annotation described there, learners request the type of assistance they need only when they want it, and are not distracted by unnecessary help materials. On the other hand, students who wish to delve more deeply into certain aspects of the reading can be given access to a veritable reader's encyclopedia of information.

Modeling

Modeling refers to attempts to assist students in two main ways: by demonstrating how to improve their general approach to reading, and by showing how to attack specific difficulties in particular reading situations. In essence, modeling represents a focus on the strategies used by skilled readers (compare the discussion in Ch. 6, "Creating Environments for Interaction," of a similar type of modeling for oral language). Transparency and learner control are again important factors in CALL modeling programs, but a third key characteristic here is the process orientation of the computer medium.

One example of an effective general pre-reading strategy is surveying. Instead of simply starting to read a passage at the beginning and proceeding steadily through in a linear fashion, many skilled readers conduct a quick preliminary survey. They flip rapidly through the pages of the passage, reading the titles and other section headings, and glancing at any diagrams, pictures, or other graphics. In this way, they establish a meaningful overall context or framework in which to interpret and fit the passage contents as they begin reading. As a second example, a useful post-reading strategy to check understanding is to construct an informal outline of the passage or of important sections (Wyatt, 1984b).

Perhaps the most common instance of a specific reading difficulty is dealing with unfamiliar vocabulary. A number of different strategies can be used in combination here, such as looking for morphological clues and deducing meaning from context (Woytak, 1984). A second example is difficulty in understanding the meaning of sentences with unusually complicated structures. One strategy advocated here is trying mentally to divide the problem sentence into two or more simpler sentences.

Both general and specific reading strategies have received attention in some reading textbooks. However, demonstrating just a few of these strategies with one reading passage takes up a large amount of space, tending to dwarf the actual reading material. With strategies such as deduction of meaning from context, the "difficult" words are the author's fixed selections, not genuine learner problems. In short, the print medium is hamstrung by its lack of transparency and learner control. The computer medium again offers a quantum leap forward in these areas. CALL reading passages will remain free of help or practice modeling materials until requests for specific types of assistance are made by individual students.

The process orientation of the computer medium gives it another important advantage over print. Deducing the meaning of an unfamiliar word from context is essentially a multiple step process. Are there clear morphological clues, such as a familiar prefix, suffix, or stem? Are there modifiers, verbs, or other elements within the clause that clearly limit the possible range of meanings? These questions form part of the process of deduction.

In print, demonstrating the process in its true multi-step form takes up a relatively large amount of space for just a few fixed examples and practice items. On the computer screen, however, this kind of demonstration—the modeling of how a skilled reader would try to deduce the meaning of a word from context—can be provided on demand for *every relevant word in every reading passage.* The same is true for all the other general and specific reading strategies. Instead of merely practicing with a fixed, limited set of examples without follow-through to authentic reading situations, students could routinely call on the computer to provide models of how to attack actual problems in the course of authentic readings.

Creative Reading

Creative reading and **adventure reading** take advantage of two further characteristics of the computer—its ability to interact with the reader and to branch rather than to follow a fixed sequence of events. One type of creative reading activity begins by asking readers for personal information. The initial questions will depend on the plot of the reading that will follow; they may ask for data such as the reader's name, age, names of relatives, pets, and the like. Of course, readers may choose to respond with imaginary information. The reading passage then begins, with the reader's name and other information figuring prominently in the story line. Typically, after presenting one or two paragraphs of the story, the computer asks the reader to choose one of several possible directions for the plot. The computer then branches to the option chosen by the reader and continues with that version of the story, stopping again for further choices.

The concepts behind creative reading have clear ties to the Language Experience Approach (LEA). In an integrated curriculum, it would be logical to follow a creative reading passage with an opportunity for learners to write their own branching stories. Simple story authoring programs (see Ch. 1, "Authoring Languages and Systems," for a description of authoring programs of various types) already make this possible.

It might be assumed that the creative reading approach requires the computer medium for its implementation, but this is not entirely the case. Using the page-jumping techniques of print medium programmed instruction, **twist-a-plot** books have enjoyed a persistent though limited popularity. However, the computer greatly enhances the branching capabilities of this reading format and offers the entirely new potential for personalization of the story line.

Adventure Reading

Adventure reading also takes advantage of the computer's ability to interact with the reader and to branch. Here, however, the branching capability is so richly exploited that it can be viewed as representing a distinct feature of the computer medium—multidimensionality.

In one common scenario for an adventure reading program, the reader plays the role of detective. The scene is a house in which a murder has recently been committed. The reader must move from room to room inside the house, looking for clues that will identify the murderer. Time is limited; the longer the investigation takes, the more likely that the murderer will be able to arrange an "accident" to eliminate the detective.

Through the interactive capability of the computer, readers are essentially in full control of their actions. They type instructions, telling the program what they want to do next ("go to the kitchen," "open the drawer," "look at the knife"). After each command, the computer responds by describing on its screen the new location reached or the results of the action. The linguistic complexity of the description can be matched to the student's reading level. Students must read closely and fully understand their situation in order to make the right next move. With well-designed adventure programs, learners often become tremendously absorbed in the reading task for impressively long periods.

An important characteristic of adventure reading is the multi-dimensional freedom of movement—any reasonable action is permitted, and readers can retrace their steps at any time. In essence, this is a specialized type of computer-based microworld (Papert, 1980b). Adventure reading programs have no equivalent in non-computer media. However, work is in progress on programs which also incorporate computer-controlled interactive video.

It should be noted that many of the commercial programs known as "interactive fiction" have all of the features of adventure reading. However, some interactive fiction software is linear in nature, and in a few cases commercial programs are closer to the creative reading paradigm. Unfortunately, most of the commercial software, whether adventure or creative reading, is unsuitable for pedagogical purposes for various reasons such as the esoteric nature of much of its vocabulary.

Figure 1 summarizes the distinctive capabilities of the computer medium, as described above, which are relevant to reading skills.

4.6   Some Problems with Computer-Assisted Reading

Hardware and Software Problems

Most of the hardware and software problems mentioned in this paper are clearly temporary. In the short term, good reading courseware will continue to be in short supply. The hardware needed for some applications, such as CD–ROM devices, is currently rather expensive; but we can expect, based on past experience with hardware in this domain, that the price will drop as demand for this type of device increases.

One factor may continue to demand consideration in CALL reading projects—the video display. The older types of microcomputer monitors, such as those used with the Apple II and IBM PC, are particularly limited. They cannot display more than half a page of text and are generally designed to produce light letters on a dark background, the reverse of a printed page. On a formal level, some research evidence suggests that reading from a screen display is less accurate and efficient than reading printed materials. Based on informal experience, certain users appear to find it stressful to read from video screens for extended periods.

With the less sophisticated monitors designed for many popular brands of microcomputers, it seems clear that the presentation of extended passages on the screen should be avoided. These video displays are therefore not particularly appropriate for reading laboratory software. However, the video displays of educationally oriented mainframe computer systems such as PLATO, TICCIT and WICAT, and the newest generation of powerful general-purpose computers offer text display capabilities which rival or exceed those of the typical printed page. The coming generation of student users is far more accustomed to working with and reading information from computer screens, and some of the newer systems present text in the familiar form of dark letters on a light background.

In any case, there are at least two ways of circumventing any problem of extended reading from the screen. With applications such as annotation, the basic reading passages are limited in number

DISTINCTIVE CAPABILITY OF COMPUTER MEDIUM	APPLICATIONS OF CAPABILITY IN READING	CLOSEST CAPABILITY IN OTHER MEDIA
–Enormous storage capacity for readings; rapid retrieval for screen display and/or printing	–Automated reading laboratory –Higher level reading skills	–Printed card reading laboratory –Not attempted in other media
–Extensive control over speed, position and way text is added	–Faster and more efficient reading	–Tachistoscope
–Dynamic screen display permitting illustrative text and graphics to be superimposed on screen	–Annotation –Modeling –Higher level reading skills	–Fixed glossaries, marginalia, notes –Rare, limited text illustrations –Occasional examples in texts of diagrams superimposed on readings
–Interaction with reader; branching capabilities allowing reader to shape reading passage	–Plot development –Adventure reading (interactive fiction)	–Programmed books –Not attempted in other media
–Individualization, self-pacing and automatic recordkeeping to manage student work	–Virtually all types of reading courseware	–Very limited in other media; the only serious attempt is printed card reading lab

Figure 1. Distinctive Capabilities of the Computer Medium Relevant to Reading Skills

and can be provided in the form of printed booklets. Accompanying CALL programs would provide complete duplicates of the passages on the screen, allowing easy access to the extensive HELP facilities.

Other applications such as reading laboratories rely on the computer's ability to provide a vast range of different reading materials and versions, a capability that cannot be matched in the print medium. In principle, the solution to this problem is simple—all that is needed is the capability to quickly and quietly print a high-quality copy of the passage or version required for each student. This approach, an example of "publishing on demand," has already been realized in the form of modern laser printers. Although today relatively expensive as compared to other printers, these are likely to fall rapidly in cost and become the dominant type of printer within the next two years.

Problems of Pedagogical Approach

Within the language teaching profession, the question of whether computers have any place in language learning is far from settled. There is a vocal minority which would reject them entirely, while a relatively large number of teachers—perhaps a majority—is not yet convinced of their value. As argued elsewhere (Wyatt, 1984c), much of the debate may be based on false premises. In the vast majority of language courses, various types of drill and metalinguistic explanation still form part of the teacher's classroom repertoire. The computer-assisted equivalents of these techniques are what I have termed instructional CALL approaches. Teachers who avoid such methods in the classroom would naturally be expected to reject courseware of this type.

However, there are two other major CALL approaches to be considered—the collaborative and facilitative approaches (see Figure 2.). These have much in common with the natural and communicative approaches to language learning (Krashen, 1981; Young, 1983). Unless CALL is inaccurately perceived as consisting entirely of instructional techniques, it is difficult to see how a blanket rejection of the computer medium can be justified, even by advocates of the natural approach.

INSTRUCTIONAL	COLLABORATIVE	FACILITATIVE
Reading laboratory	Modeling	Annotation
Higher level reading skills	Creative reading	
Faster and more efficient reading	Adventure reading	

Figure 2. Classification of CALL Reading Courseware Examples in This Paper

4.7   Conclusion

In summary, the computer remains in most respects a new medium for language learning and for the development of second and foreign language reading skills. Technological advances have already produced or will soon provide all of the hardware necessary for extremely powerful reading applications. While the potential for enhancing familiar activities and designing entirely new ones is becoming clearer, virtually none of the important reading courseware has yet been developed. And as the development process begins, the severest critics of CALL may be its best allies in keeping the primary focus where it should be—squarely on pedagogical considerations.

Writing

5 Computers, Composition, and Second Language Teaching

Marianne Phinney

5.1 Introduction

The last decade has seen two revolutions in composition instruction. Research and practice in English composition has turned from the influence of rhetorical models to emphasis on the writing process (Emig, 1971; Flower and Hayes, 1981; Perl, 1979; Sommers, 1980). In the last five years, composition teachers and researchers have also discovered a new tool for composing and revision—the microcomputer. Work on the effects of the computer on student writing processes, revision, attitudes toward writing, and student written products has exploded, with a computer search turning up over seventy citations in the last two years alone. Yet the computer revolution seems to have barely touched second language composing research.

Although the process approach to composition teaching has begun to filter into second language teaching, it appears from the literature that computer use in the second language composition classroom is still in its infancy. This is unfortunate; second language students can derive many of the same benefits from computer-assisted composition as native language writers, and possibly more.

Research on the composing process with writers in English as a Second Language (ESL) has suggested that non-native writers approach the writing process similarly to native writers (Lay, 1982; Raimes, 1983; Spack, 1984; Zamel, 1983, 1987). The writing process is not linear, as presented by many writing texts for both native and non-native writers; writing is a discovery process, for finding out what the writer wants to say (Emig, 1971), and is recursive (Murray, 1980). Novice native writers, however, often view writing as a mechanical skill, and as product-focused (Perl, 1979; Sommers, 1980). They may have trouble generating enough content as a basis for writing, or may suffer from writer's block stemming from too rigid a view of the writing process (Rose, 1984). Unskilled writers tend to focus on surface editing rather than structural revisions; they will edit more locally and more readily than will experienced writers, who view the text as mutable and fluid (Sommers, 1980).

Non-native writers seem to have many of the same concerns about writing. Perhaps because of the traditional emphasis on grammar and correctness in many language classes and textbooks, second language students are often concerned with accuracy. Their perception of the importance of the structure of the product may also stem from previous writing experience. Bilingual writers also suffer from similar sources of writer's block as do monolinguals (Betancourt and Phinney, 1988).

Raimes (1987) presents a detailed think-aloud protocol study of remedial and non-remedial ESL writers and compares them with a similar study of native writers (Pianko, 1979). She reports that composing strategies are similar in L2 and L1 writers, although her ESL students showed less tendency to prematurely edit and more rehearsal for ideas and language use than Pianko's L1 writers. Like naive L1 writers, her ESL students tended to become stuck with their text once it was written, and invoked general abstract rules about form and essay structure before generating content. She does suggest teaching rehearsal techniques, since her students seemed to use them to experiment with options in their texts.

Proficient ESL writers use many of the same strategies used by native writers. Zamel (1982, 1983) found that students varied from an outliner who made lexical and syntactic revisions to students who radically restructured first drafts. All of the students Zamel interviewed indicated that the writing and discovery processes went hand in hand. Basic ESL writers, however, also suffer from the same problems as basic native writers (Raimes, 1983; Spack, 1984) and can be taught to use similar techniques to overcome their difficulties (Johns, 1986).

Given the similarity between the prewriting and possibly the revision stages for native and non-native writers, Zamel (1976, 1987) has argued strongly that second language composition teaching needs to adopt the findings and techniques of native composition research. Although not all second language writing teachers have adopted a process approach, for various reasons, it is clear that both students and teachers benefit from an approach to writing that is content-based, with less emphasis on rules for writing (either negative or positive) and more emphasis on writing for meaning. In this vein, second language composition teachers and students can also benefit from what has been found about the effects of computer-assisted composition with native writers.

5.2   Computer-Assisted Composition and Novice Writers

Although the computer has been used in composition classes for several years, frequently it has been relegated to a drill-and-practice tutor for grammar exercises, sentence combining, and similar types of objective exercises (Wresch, 1984). Current approaches, however, concentrate on word processing and other process-oriented activities. It is these I will focus on, since drill-and-practice programs have more relevance for language and grammar classes than for second language writing classes.

Computers and Writing in the Native Language

Research on the effects of computer use in composition has primarily consisted of case studies (Nichols, 1986; Womble, 1984) and anecdotal reports (Doggrell, 1986; Hunter, 1984; Schwartz, 1982), with a few controlled studies beginning to appear (Lutz, 1987). Because of the wide variety of student responses to both writing and the computer, experimental and statistical studies which compare groups rather than individuals often produce less than spectacular results (Phinney, 1988). Nevertheless, certain findings have consistently recurred in the literature.

The first few studies were generally small and anecdotal, usually reported by the instructor of the class. The researcher was often a fervent convert to word processing, and some of the earlier papers have an almost proselytizing tone (e.g., Schwartz claims "writing becomes a playground where revising is part of the fun instead of part of the punishment" 1984, p. 240). In spite of some mixed results, studies suggested that using word processing made revision easier, resulting in more and different types of revisions (Bean, 1983; Bradley, 1982, Hunter, 1984; Monohan, 1982; Womble, 1984); altered revision behavior (Bradley, 1982; Hunter, 1984; Madigan, 1984, Monohan, 1982; Schwartz, 1982); increased time spent in writing (Nichols, 1986; Womble, 1984); overcame blocking and allowed students to be objective about their writing (Daiute, 1983, 1985); and improved attitudes toward writing (Daiute, 1985; Phinney and Mathis, 1987, in preparation; Schwartz, 1982; Schwartz, 1984)

Much of the initial enthusiasm about word processing in the composition classroom came from professional writers who were delighted with their new tool. Madigan (1984) claimed that the word processor itself would alter writing behavior, partly based on his own experience. Teachers soon learned, however, that changes in student writing behavior came slowly, if at all, and were dependent on the amount of time available with the machine and the amount of writing achieved. While some studies reported changes in student revision behavior (Madigan, 1984; Monohan, 1982; Schwartz 1982, 1984) others reported no significant changes (Collier, 1983). In some cases, the lack of effect can be attributed to the program used (Pufahl, 1984) or to a short exposure time for the students.

More recent studies, however, have confirmed that students do not generally take advantage of the computer's capabilities for revision. Inexperienced writers, whether they are writing in their first or second language, tend to have the most trouble with revision. They often focus on surface changes, editing rather than revising, or rewrite a text entirely without reference to earlier drafts (Sommers, 1980). Writing on a computer, then, poses two problems: dealing with a new technology and at the same time trying to do something which requires special skills.

Even when teachers emphasize the computer's facilities for revision, such as **block moves** and **delete functions**, use of **fact files**, **note files**, and other "cut and paste" techniques, students more often use the computer for **microrevision** rather than for **macrorevision**. Many studies have reported that some students revised less when they worked on a computer than when they wrote by hand (Daiute, 1986; Benesch, 1987; Harris, 1985). Although basic writers and ESL writers can certainly be taught techniques to help them invent (Blanton, 1987; Spack, 1984) and revise extensively (Daiute, 1985; Johns, 1986), using a computer alone does not seem to stimulate different revision behavior, although students may produce more "drafts" (hard copies).

It may be, in fact, that the structure of word processing programs does not easily lend itself to macrorevision, even with the text alteration facilities available (Neuman and Cobb-Morocco, 1987–88). There are significant differences between revising with a hard copy and revising on-line which may push the writer toward one type of revision. With a hard copy, whether printed, typed, or hand-written, the entire text is available to the writer; on a computer, a page or less is displayed at any given time. This may in fact lead to focusing on minor changes (Lutz, 1987).

To go to another part of the text often requires paging back or forward through the text, a process which is still slower than flipping pages by hand. This seems to affect the way people view the text. Haas and Hayes (1986), in their study of experienced computer users, found that subjects had more problems remembering where information occurred in the text, finding errors, and evaluating texts when they were on screen than when they were in printed form. Other studies have noted that most computer users rely on hard copy, produce more hard copies than non-computer users, and still use standard marking and cut-and-paste techniques for substantive revisions (Harris, 1985). When experienced writers who have been using computers for some time still report such difficulties, we should not be surprised when our students do not immediately alter their revision behavior.

The greatest effect of computer-assisted composition appears to be the change of attitudes toward writing. Almost every study has reported that students enjoy using a computer to write and that they feel a sense of mastery and accomplishment in learning to use the software. Students often spend more time writing when they use a computer (Nichols, 1986; Womble, 1984), apparently because they enjoy it. In the program at the University of Texas at El Paso, classes are taught in the computer laboratory, and students often stay after class to continue writing as well as coming in during non-class hours. When interviewed, students say they write more, that their papers are better, and also that they enjoy writing more than by hand—statements which hold true for ESL students as well (Benesch, 1987; Phinney and Mathis, in preparation).

Computers and Writing in the Second Language

As with research on writing processes, research on using computers to write in a second language has lagged behind the native language research. Much of the research is still anecdotal or based on case-studies. Piper (1987), observing intermediate ESL students whose class met in a microcomputer lab, noted that although they were encouraged to work together on the computer, not all the students enjoyed group work; many, especially those who did not like using the computer, preferred to work alone. Her students felt that learning word processing was useful, a modern way to write, and motivated them to write more, although some students dropped out because they felt intimidated or distracted by the computer.

Benesch (1987) reported a case study of three ESL students, all of whom were revisers with pen and paper. She, too, noted that none of her students used the computer to revise, even the one who had previously revised extensively. She also reported varying reactions to the computer; one student focused on surface editing, one used the computer for content generation and discovery, and the third, an avowed technophobe, concentrated on adapting to the computer as technology. All ultimately responded positively to the computer and felt they learned by using it to write.

Phinney and Mathis (1987, in preparation) interviewed a dozen ESL students taking freshman composition in a computer lab. While the course had a high attrition rate for the same reasons noted by Piper (1987), the students who completed the course all agreed that using the computer made their work load easier. Most students also indicated that they enjoyed writing more, felt they wrote better in English and expressed less fear about writing in English. Not all students agreed, certainly; one student who hated writing when he began still hated it at the end, and another student, an older woman, had tremendous problems adapting to the mechanical aspects of the computer, but stuck with it doggedly to the end. Although Phinney and Mathis (1987) reported significant increases in length and improvements in accuracy as measured by error-free T-units, they were not compared to similar non-computer users, so it is impossible to say whether the improvements were due to computer use.

The benefits of using a computer to write, far from being as wide-reaching as originally hoped, have turned out to be more modest. Improvement in the affective factors of attitudes toward English and toward writing, motivation to write, time spent writing, and perceptions about one's writing behavior appear to be the major benefits of computer-assisted writing. For second language students, the computer also appears to reduce the fear of errors and to reduce worries about legibility (Berens, 1986b; Piper, 1987). However, without specific instruction in using the computer to facilitate the writing process, from prewriting to revision, the computer alone appears to have little effect in changing writing behavior in naive writers (Daiute, 1986; Rodrigues, 1985), whether they are writing in their first or second language.

5.3   Computers as Writing Aids

Improved attitudes toward English and writing is certainly a laudable goal, worth pursuing with electronic aids, but is it sufficient to justify the expense of setting up a computer writing lab and training teachers in the use of the new technology? Fortunately, the computer can also serve as conference partner, audience, and to a lesser extent, critic as well as the center for peer reading and editing. In spite of the traditional view of the computer as a drill-and-practice tutor, it can also participate with the student in an open-ended dialogue about the text at any stage from prewriting to revision (Fischer and Fischer, 1985; Rodrigues and Rodrigues, 1986). For students writing in their second language, these abilities are particularly useful when they are tailored to meet individual needs.

Exploiting the Word Processor

Since basic writers and second language writers, who have much in common, often do not immediately see the possibilities inherent in the word processing program for composing and revision, they should be given careful instruction on exploiting the computer (Berens, 1986a, 1986b; Phinney, 1987; Rodrigues, 1985). This can often be done simply with a word processing program and disk-based exercise files (Williams, 1987). Such files often function as templates, providing writing heuristics, suggestions for strategies in content generation and organization, revision and editing exercises, and exercises which teach various aspects of the software. These files often resemble a good writing workbook or exercise book, but with an important difference: the student can answer the questions, then save the file for later use. The questions can be deleted and the answers used as a basis for further writing or revision without the need to recopy the information.

For non-native writers, such files can be particularly helpful. They can lead the student to rehearse different approaches to the same topic, as suggested by Raimes (1987), or provide guidelines for writing or checklists for linguistic problems. While non-native students will use such heuristics when writing by hand, they are enhanced by the computer's natural attraction. Other pen and pencil techniques can be easily adapted to a more interactive screen mode (Williams, 1987).

Almost anything that can be done with pencil and paper can be transferred to a computer, with the exception of brain patterns or clusters (Hughey, Wormuth, Harfiel, and Jacobs, 1983: 64–66.). **Nutshelling, freewriting, invisible writing** (Marcus and Blau, 1983), **listing, idea files,** and **notecards** can all be typed directly into word processing files which are then available for expansion and further composition. Some students may even choose to write their journals on the computer if they have access.

Question heuristics, dialogue templates, "forgery" exercises and **incomplete texts** (Newman, 1987), as well as various types of **planners**, can all be prepared by the instructor and placed on a general work disk for students to copy or on the server of a network. Figure 1 provides an illustration of a prewriting template based on Blum, Brinkman, Hoffman, and Peck (1984).

Similar instructions for organizing, commenting, and peer commenting can also be left on files for students.

Commercial Productivity Software for Composition

With the increased interest in computers in composition, more software developers have issued specialized packages for use in writing. These can include commercial productivity software for writing, such as an **idea processor, spelling checker, thesaurus, style checker** and **grammar checker**. Unfortunately, while many word processors can be used for writing in languages other than English, most productivity software is available only in English. This limits their usefulness in classes for languages other than ESL.

EXPLORE YOUR TOPIC

Welcome to this exploration file! Answer the questions to explore what you know about your topic. This will give you material to help find a main point and make a rough plan. When you have answered the questions, save this file under a different name on your disk. What is your topic? State it briefly.

Now answer the following questions about your topic. If you think one of the questions does not apply, write "DOES NOT APPLY" after the question.

WHO is involved in your topic?
WHAT things are involved?
WHEN does the topic happen?
WHERE does the topic take place?
WHY does the topic happen?
HOW does the topic happen?

What can you DESCRIBE about your topic?
What CHANGES have occurred in it?
Can you relate an INCIDENT about it?
What do you REMEMBER about it?
What are its PARTS, SECTIONS, or ELEMENTS?
Can you give INSTRUCTIONS for making or doing it?
How do you RESPOND to it or FEEL about it?
Why is it VALUABLE or IMPORTANT?
What CAUSES it?
What RESULTS from it?
Can you clarify it by COMPARING it to something?
Are you FOR or AGAINST it? Why?

Save this file and print out a copy of it. Then go to the READ AND ANALYZE file to help you find a main point for your paper.

Figure 1. Heuristics Template Based on Blum et al. (1984)

TITLE: PERSUASIVE PAPER PLANNER

− Topic

− Existing facts

+ Opinion

      + Reason #1 for your opinion
        − evidence (fact)
        − evidence (anecdote)
        − evidence (details)
        − evidence (reason)
      + Reason #2 for your opinion
        − evidence (fact)
        − evidence (anecdote)
        − evidence (details)
        − evidence (reason)
      + Reason #3 for your opinion
        − evidence (fact)
        − evidence (anecdote)
        − evidence (details)
        − evidence (reason)
      + Opposing point of view
        − evidence for opposing view
        − counterarguments

+ Restate opinion

      − summarize arguments
      − further incident in support
      − concluding statement

Figure 2. Persuasive Paper Template for Idea Processor (Outliner)

Idea processors, as the name implies, provide ways to record ideas and organize them into some form of outline. Many allow the writer to rank items in order of importance, hide items, expand them to paragraphs, and reorder items to restructure the outline. In a composition class, idea processors may be a luxury expense. Much can be done with outlining using the word processor, and idea processors tend to lead the writer into a linear order which may be uncomfortable for some students. Although instructional templates can be designed for these programs, as illustrated in Figure 2, the same templates can probably be used as profitably with the word processor.

Of the productivity software, the most useful to second language writers is a spelling checker or a thesaurus. Most ESL students feel unsure about spelling in English; a spelling checker relieves some of that anxiety. By restricting use of the speller to next-to-final or final drafts, students can also be induced to leave spelling concerns to the final edit, thus reducing preediting. In many programs, a speller is available at any time during the writing process, and is of the type which, when a word is not found, presents alternative spellings in a window over the text. Since students learning a second language often find they can recognize the correct spelling even when they are not sure how to produce it, the spelling checker allows them to reduce errors without tedium. It does not alleviate the need for a dictionary since the computer's choices are not always correct, but it speeds up the correction process. Very often, the choices will alert students to the fact that they have chosen the wrong word as well.

Many students also find the thesaurus useful, particularly the more advanced students who are sensitive to shades of meaning in words. Here again, students should be cautioned about blind acceptance of computer choices; a monolingual dictionary should be at hand to confirm the meaning of the words selected. The thesaurus, like its printed counterpart, is used less than the speller (dictionary), since it requires openness to options and differences in meaning. Many students with limited English proficiency and little writing experience tend to view what they have written as immutable at first.

Grammar and style checkers, if not included as part of a writing package, tend to be less useful for second language writers for a number of reasons. Many are not very productive for first language writers (Raskin, 1986); they often provide totally inappropriate responses to second language prose simply because the language problems are at a much lower level. Many of these programs provide statistical analyses of readability, sentence length, average word length, frequency word counts, and counts of specific items such as *be* verbs and prepositions. They also may search for inappropriate language (e.g., sexist language, vague terms, commonly misused words such as *lay/lie*, and trite phrases).

For experienced writers working in their native language, these programs often help the writer find potential style and grammar problems. For basic non-native writers, the advice given is often inappropriate and misleading. For example, a program which highlights every gender-marked pronoun and tells the student to watch out for sexist language is not much help when the problem is not sexism but overuse of pronouns without referents or switching of *he* and *she*. Reid (1987) reported that ESL students who used a commercially available grammar and style checker found that only a few of the programs were worthwhile. Even experienced writers know that the advice given by these programs must be taken with a grain of salt; non-native writers should be counseled to consider the suggestions carefully (Berens, 1986b) and understand that the computer cannot *read* the text, but only counts it.

A better approach might be to set up exercise files or work pages to help students with common errors. For example, a SEARCH function could be used to find all instances of *the*; at each find, the student can be told to check the phrase to see if the article is used correctly. Similar techniques can be used with prepositions, common two-place verbs, specialized vocabulary problems, pronouns, and overused vague words such as *something*. A worksheet which helps students make a copy of the text file, highlight topic sentences, move them to the beginning of the file, and place them into an outline might be just as effective in helping organization problems as an idea processor.

Process-Prompting Programs

Perhaps the greatest potential lies in software designed especially to teach the writing process. This software, which often uses dialogue heuristics for prewriting, content generation, organization, and revision, allows the computer to act as a partner in a writing conference

(Burns and Culp, 1980; Huntley, 1986; Rodrigues and Rodrigues, 1984; Schwartz, 1984; Wresch, 1982, 1984). These programs differ from the activity files described above in that they are interactive and often incorporate aspects of the student's responses (topic or phrases) into the questions.

Although research comparing use of these programs to word processing or longhand writing is only beginning, one study indicates that they can help students revise substantially beyond the micro level (Daiute, 1986). Although her junior high school students did not revise extensively when using word processing as compared to writing by hand, they did show significantly more revisions and a wider range of revisions (micro to macro) when they used a prompting program (Daiute, 1985).

Such prompting programs help the student recall the steps involved in writing, stimulate content generation, and help students focus on aspects of their writing that need revising. There are several of these programs currently on the market for use in English writing. Most of them use a language level which is appropriate for high intermediate to advanced proficiency ESL writers, and they can be used profitably to aid prewriting and macro revision.

Some of these programs also contain mini-style checkers. Like the commercial productivity software described above, these programs often fail second language writers in focusing on problems which are beyond the level of the writer and ignoring problems which are endemic to second language writing, such as misuse of prepositions and articles, false cognates, inappropriate language level, and use of idioms. Some programs come with customization routines which allow the instructor to set up original files; these could be directed to the needs of ESL or other second language students.

5.4   The Computer in the Writing Workshop

A computer laboratory also provides a productive environment for **writing workshops, peer review**, and **class publishing** (Sudol, 1985). The screen display is at once private and public. Students very often feel that the printed display allows them to concentrate on their work (Phinney and Mathis, in preparation; Schwartz, 1982; Womble, 1984) and some feel a sense of privacy about their writing; one student noted that if he wrote anything he did not like, he could erase it without embarrassment (Rodrigues, 1985). In another sense the screen is public. Anyone standing behind the writer can read the text easily, yet the writer need not be disturbed.

This greatly facilitates conferencing and peer commenting. Students can share a monitor or work closely enough to see each other's monitors and comment on the work in progress. Williams (1987) even suggests swapping the monitors while they write. The printed style of the display allows both reviewer and writer to spot needed changes easily. Conducting a teacher-student conference on a computer is much easier; the teacher can comment verbally on the text without removing it from the student's view, as so often happens when the text is handwritten. Often, revisions can be incorporated immediately. Second language students in particular seem to appreciate this kind of interaction; the instructor's presence assures them that the revision will be appropriate and that errors **can be corrected right away**.

Peer commenting can also be enhanced with the computer. Using a copy of a students' file, other students can insert comments, suitably marked so that the writer can find them—e.g., in capitals, parentheses, marked with asterisks, etc. (Rodrigues and Rodrigues, 1986). The writer can retrieve this copy and revise directly, or print it out and revise the original. If the computers are linked via a network, central comment templates and files can be accessible to the entire class.

Collaborative writing is also simple to implement with computers. Shared files or merged files provide an easy way to blend the work of two writers into a single text. The resulting printout looks like the work of a team rather than the individuals implied in handwritten copies. It can lead to class publication as well. The first semester in which computers were used in ESL freshman composition at the University of Texas at El Paso, students collaborated on a lab manual describing the basic procedures for using the machines and the software in the lab. That manual was printed and sold to students the following semester, and is still in use.

5.5   Conclusion

Students can learn to use the computer to write in a second language, but we cannot expect rapid changes in their writing behavior. Since writing skills transfer from first to second language (Raimes, 1987), those students who are basic writers in their first language will also be basic writers in their second language. Acquisition of writing skills is a complex process which takes time; when the novel technology of the computer is added, there seems to be a lag as students master the new techniques enough to continue writing. Often it seems that students backslide in their writing behavior as they struggle with the machine. It may take months or even years for the computer to change their writing behavior.

Evidence from both native and non-native writers indicate that the computer is not a panacea for basic writing problems. The machine and software are tools, nothing more. Students should be introduced to the computer and software gradually, on a "need to know" basis, to allow them to concentrate on the writing rather than the technology. I have also found that it pays to introduce one piece of software at a time; let them become functional with the word processor before adding spellers or other programs. This also forces students to focus on completing their writing before using editing aids. Berens (1986b) suggests that students not be required to use the computer; certain sections can be designated as computer use sections, so students can choose.

I have also found, as have others (Daiute, 1985, 1986; Johns, 1986), that students need to be taught revision strategies that are appropriate to word processing. I encourage revision on a hard copy, but must demonstrate how to make the changes on the printout, then on the computer; otherwise several students try to rewrite their paper by hand and then type it again on the machine. Most students also need hints on storage of files, including using mnemonic file names as well as different file names for each draft.

When considering commercially developed software for non-native students, we often must rely on packages designed for native writers. Depending on the language proficiency and writing experience of our students, certain aspects of the software are crucial. First and foremost, software should be **user-friendly** and come with a self-paced tutorial. If the students have a beginning to intermediate level proficiency, we cannot depend on the software manuals to instruct them. Many instructors write their own simplified instructions for non-native students; I prefer to rely on on-line instruction whenever possible. The best software does not require the manual; on-screen help screens and instructions allow students with a minimum of computer literacy to figure out basic functions. It is also much easier to demonstrate such programs to students. If the commands are minimal and available on-screen during writing or at the touch of one or two keys, then students can concentrate on writing and not on learning the software.

In the long run, students writing on computers will catch up to traditional students and perhaps surpass them. They will also have improved attitudes about writing and about the second language as well as a new skill to show for it. With these more modest expectations, the integration of the computer into second language composition can be an important factor in the growth of our students as language users and writers.

Speaking/Listening

6 Applications of Computers in the Development of Speaking and Listening Proficiency

Martha C. Pennington

6.1 Introduction

Every medium is a unique **symbol system**, that is, a unique set of symbols and capacities for structuring and presenting information. As a result, each medium has a unique potential for impacting on learning and cognition (Pennington, 1985; Salomon, 1979). The computer, which can run a great variety of types of programs and which can link up with a wide array of peripheral devices, is an especially versatile medium, or set of media (as described in Ch. 1, "Hardware Input/Output"). In fact, the computer can incorporate within its sweeping umbrella of operations and potentials virtually all other media and their unique properties. Moreover, it allows for the juxtaposition of two or more symbol systems, such as oral and pictorial or written and pictorial, "in a way that encourages the user to translate concepts from one system to the other" (Dickson, 1985). In this respect, the computer has a potential for altering the learning behavior of users by helping them to develop new perspectives on a certain body of information and new approaches to comprehending and organizing experience.

In addition to the features it shares with other media, the computer provides the unique capabilities of vast storage capacity within a small space and certain types of mechanical operations that allow it to store, manipulate and analyze great quantities of data very rapidly. When all of these capabilities come together in one device, we have a very powerful medium indeed, one offering tremendous creative resources for education. Thus, it is logical to ask how this

medium can best be used in a language curriculum to enhance other
activities aimed at the development of proficiency in the four skill
areas of reading, writing, speaking and listening. The applications to
the text-based skills of reading and writing are perhaps more obvious
than the applications to speaking and listening, and, there seems in
fact to have been a greater effort in software development up to now
in the text-based as opposed to the speech-based aspects of the oral
language curriculum.

The utility of computers in the oral language curriculum is in
fact no less natural, and no less significant, than in the text-based
curriculum. Like other media such as audiotape recordings or books,
computers have two broad ways of providing instruction in speaking and listening: (1) they can create environments which facilitate
interaction, and (2) they can provide training in production and
perception of speech. Also like various other media, computers offer
opportunities for conducting research and for testing student performance in the speech-based aspects of the language curriculum. Some
of the roles of computers in language instruction are similar to those
played by traditional media and may not represent advances over
those media; some roles offer definite improvements over traditional
ways of providing instruction; still others could not be realized at all
by means of traditional media.

In what follows, the various roles which computers can play in
communicative interaction, training, research and testing for speech-
based language are explored. The chapter begins with a classification
of the types of skills which make up speaking and listening proficiency in both meaningful and mechanical aspects. Then, the types
of activities relevant for working on speaking and listening skills are
classified into task-types. For each task-type, traditional instructional modalities vs. computer-based instruction are examined and
contrasted. It is seen how computers compare to traditional approaches in the delivery of instruction and in the provision of opportunities to develop speech-based communicative skills. In this way,
the unique strengths of the computer medium for working on speaking and listening skills are set in sharper relief against a background
of the capabilities of traditional media. The last major section of
the paper addresses the ways in which computers can be applied to
assessment of and research on the listening and speaking skills of
second or foreign language learners.

6.2   Components of Speaking and Listening Proficiency

The meaningful domain of speaking/listening proficiency is meant to include **the grammar of oral language** and various aspects of the "rules of speaking" subsumed in the second language literature under such categories as **language functions, cultural appropriateness,** and **conversational strategies.** In addition to these meaningful dimensions of communication, the speaker needs to master certain mechanical distinctions in the pronunciation of a language in order to become a competent speaker and listener. These include the **articulatory and acoustic parameters** which uniquely define and identify the individual sounds, or phonemes, of a particular language as against all others and which are the basis for listening acuity and articulatory precision. They also include the overall features of stretches of speech termed **voice quality** (Laver, 1980; Esling and Wong, 1983), **prosody** and **fluent speech** phenomena. As stressed in Pennington and Richards (1986), voice quality and other features of speech which span more than one segment, so-called **suprasegmental** features, are essential to natural-sounding speech in a second or foreign language.

The meaningful and mechanical domains of speech are often treated separately in language courses. It may be valuable to work on the articulation and discrimination of individual sounds or patterns of sounds at least partly in isolation from their meaningful contexts. Such training may help to focus the learner's attention on the criterial features of the pronunciation of the second or foreign language without the distraction or pressure of trying to construct or to comprehend speech in meaningful contexts. At the same time, it is possible to tie work on articulation and discrimination of segments or stretches of speech to meaningful contexts, as, for example, when an exercise requires a student to pay special attention to reduced forms (e.g., contractions) in colloquial speech or to a certain sound contrast in order to be able to complete a communicative task (see Pica, 1984, for examples). In this vein, activities can be devised which require students to mimic or to identify voice characteristics or intonational patterns associated with certain language functions, culturally appropriate messages or interactions between specific types of participants. Ways to use the computer to work on the meaningful and the mechanical dimensions of speech both separately and jointly are explored below.

6.3   Ways to Develop Oral Language: How Does the Computer Compare to Other Approaches?

Task-Types for Oral Language Development

Classroom activities for working directly on oral language can be classified into five task-types: **free conversation**; **directed discussion** based on problem-solving, information gap activities and other pair or small group activities which require discussion and negotiation of meaning; **situational simulation**, or role-play; **highly structured conversation-based activities** such as dialogue completion, which may or may not require actual speaking or listening (i.e., it may be a written exercise); and various types of **noninteractional speech-based activities** such as choral or individual repetition, monologues or lectures given as speeches and recorded on tape (e.g., by students for later analysis by the instructor), or used as stimuli for listening exercises (e.g., cloze passages or various types of listening comprehension exercises). Note that this last task-type, unlike the others, is not based on two-way conversational interaction.

The relationship between these task-types can be illustrated as in Figure 1.

Although the activities designated as type (4) may not involve actual speaking or listening practice, they are meant to help the student develop conversational speaking and listening skills. Type (5), in contrast, is the category for all listening or speaking activities designed to assist students in producing and comprehending material which is not based on spoken interaction between two participants.

The next section overviews the uses of computers in implementing the first four task-types to create environments for interaction with varying degrees of control. Since task-type (5) differs from the others in not being conversation-based, it will be examined in a separate later section.

	Involves Spoken Interaction	Degree of External Control of Activity
1. Free Conversation	yes	none
2. Directed Discussion	yes	little
3. Situational Simulation	yes	moderate
4. Highly Structured Conversation-Based Activities	maybe	great
5. Non-Interactional Speech-Based Activities	no	great

Figure 1. Relationship Between Five Task-Types in an Oral Language Curriculum

Creating Environments for Interaction

When a user makes contact with another user and "talks to" that person on a computer screen using a word processing or other message-generating capability, this is in a sense a kind of **free conversation**. We might also say that a writer engages in "free conversation with a computer" when using word processing as a modality for "free-writing." However, these uses of the computer are only in a very limited and metaphorical sense "conversations," in that the computer is only providing an environment for communication, not actually conversing with the user, and also in the sense that writing, even when it is an immediate response to another person or "stream-of-consciousness" narration, is far from equivalent to oral production.

Free conversation in the literal sense is a speaking format which computers at the present time are very far from being able to realize (see Ch. 1, "Natural Language and Artificial Intelligence," for discussion). It is therefore a type of speaking task best provided through the traditional "delivery systems" in language education of discussion groups or conversation partners. At the same time, conversation-like activities may be carried out by means of a computer, or conversations between two speakers may be analyzed by means of a computer, as described below.

As regards the next three task-types—**directed discussion, situational simulation,** and **highly structured conversation-based activities**—the computer has utility in creating environments which facilitate interaction, serving as a "stimulator of learner-centered activity" (de Quincy, 1986, p. 56). In some cases, these are environments which can be created without a computer, using traditional media such as textbooks or pictures. However, when such environments are created with the computer, the special characteristics associated with the machine can make them especially effective. Pennington (1986b) describes this function of computers as that of making input not only more comprehensible, but also more memorable:

> Memorable input is input which is *salient* or *striking* to the learner and, therefore, likely to make such a strong mental impression that it will be interpreted and retained in memory.... In both the sense of making information memorable and in the sense of personalizing instruction, the computer has a great potential for increasing the *accessibility* of input to students.   (p. 7)

At the same time, Pennington (1986b), citing the work of Chaudron (1985) and Richards (1986), stresses the need for language learning software to "move beyond mere novelty to the skill-based and task-based learning activities which are the focus of language pedagogy of the '80's."

Recent developments in software provide environments in which pairs or small groups of students clustered around a computer must interact in certain ways in order to accomplish particular problem solving tasks or joint projects. For example, Dickson (1985) shows how software designed to juxtapose two symbol systems "creates social encounters among learners that elicit the active use and discussion of these symbol systems" (p. 30). As one instance, Dickson (1985) describes a computer-based "referential communication game":

> In this game a set of six pictures appear on the screen. These pictures include such things as faces that are smiling or frowning or a basketball in some spatial relation-

ship to a basket (above, below, on the corner, etc.). Typically two children play the game together, with one child trying to describe a designated picture so that the other child can select it from among the others.... This game requires a translation of pictorial information in the visual display into spoken language rich in logical ("no nose and slanting eyebrows") or spatial ("near the corner on the top") language in a way that another person can accurately select the picture described.   (pp. 31–32)

Such software is necessarily interactive in that the game requires two people. That is, it is designed to create an environment for communication between at least two individuals. Moreover, as has been documented by research (Dickson 1982), this software is far more successful than some traditional modalities in generating real communication among the users:

Analysis of the language used by children in these contexts reveals a much greater frequency of use of complex linguistic forms and questions than occurs in other common classroom activities such as reading groups. For example, a comparison of the frequency of children's requests for information from peers in reading groups compared with such requests while engaged in a referential communication task showed that such requests were approximately 25 times more frequent in the referential communication activity.   (Dickson, 1985, p. 32)

It is possible to set up this kind of game without the use of a computer, e.g., by using two sets of similar but not identical picture cards. However, the computer offers advantages and variations not possible without the use of this electronic medium. First, the exact nature of the pictures can be varied for every game, so that the same users can play the same game many times without ever encountering exactly the same conditions. Second, the computer can be programmed to play against a user and to model the correct strategies for winning the game. In one variation on this type of game, the computer plays against one or more students, using stored speech cues to different pictures. Such a game offers practice in listening comprehension and at the same time can provide a model not only of the specific verbal patterns used to describe the pictures, but also of the cognitive strategies involved in forming the spoken descriptions. For example, the computer "thinks out loud" about the best way of describing a certain picture: "Hmmm. How can I describe this one? I see. I have to tell how it is different" (Dickson, 1985, p. 33). The student later takes over the computer's role in the game, playing with a second student.

Another variation on this type of program juxtaposes the same kind of visual and auditory media, while adding the element of physical manipulation of graphics. The computer gives the student directions to draw a certain figure or to move pre-drawn components to a certain place on the screen. As in the previous case, a student may later take on the computer's role, giving directions to fellow students to perform the physical manipulations.

Dickson's microcomputer "referential communication game" aids in the development of specific communicative skills, as "the visual display is deliberately designed to evoke specific linguistic forms and patterns of social interaction" (1985, p. 32). More courseware could be designed to exploit the possibilities of juxtaposing symbol systems to deliberately evoke certain types of language. Such courseware can improve or add to conversational competencies by providing an impetus for working on specific aspects of oral grammar, language functions, culturally appropriate expressions, and the patterns of "moves" and "responses" which characterize conversational exchanges.

Dickson's game and variants on his theme represent a whole class of courseware which can model language and cognitive strategies in the presence of visual stimuli that can be viewed and manipulated as the language and strategies are modeled. This combination of linguistic, cognitive, and media functions provides learning opportunities which cannot exactly be matched in other types of instructional environments. In other uses, the computer provides environments and opportunities for communication which are difficult to duplicate by means of other media within a classroom environment, thus adding substantially to the repertoire of sensory resources available to the instructor and to the students for creating learning experiences and so increasing the accessibility of meaningful input.

Joint projects requiring students to design charts using spreadsheet programs, to develop databases, to use a word processor to do collective writing, or to use graphics to create realistic or fantasized objects which perform certain functions or which have particular characteristics all provide stimulating environments for directed discussion. Games which involve clues and inferencing based on stored data are another type of problem-solving activity which can serve to facilitate specific types of interaction and language. These activities may or may not directly focus on language; whatever the content or exact goal of the activity, it will have language as a by-product.

A classroom computer also makes possible certain types of situational simulations and role-playing activities which are not achievable by other media. With the aid of computers, students become entrepreneurs, archaeologists or historians, working in groups at the computer and elsewhere to create worlds, to investigate data, to discover facts and principles, and to conduct experiments without going "on site" or placing themselves or others in the dangerous circumstances which may occur in "live" experiments.

Besides creating classroom opportunities which are difficult to duplicate without a computer, computer capabilities which extend the sensory repertoire available for instruction can be used to enhance an otherwise dull or repetitive task designed to be performed by an individual. While not able to engage in free conversation with the user, a computer can provide opportunities for highly structured conversation-based activities such as "controlled dialogue." Even drill-and-practice grammar software can become memorable by means of certain "communicative enhancements" such as those applied by Robinson (1986) to otherwise ordinary software. In a review of a widely used ESL grammar drill-and-practice program, Pennington (1984) notes some of the best features of this type of program: "We can find exercises which incorporate specific and relevant feedback; which use game-challenge features, graphics and color to enhance both grammatical presentation and practice; and which show careful attention to cross-cultural focus and reality of content and interaction" (p. 1).

With the addition of synchronized audiotape, digitized or synthesized speech enhancements (see Ch. 1, "Inputting and Outputting Sound and Video Images"), this type of courseware can provide more than an on-screen "dialog" with the user. Such software then becomes an excellent vehicle for developing listening comprehension exercises related to the grammatical focus of the lesson. Even a traditional multiple-choice exercise format, if answers are offered in audio form, can provide a stimulating environment for working—though possibly not directly, that is, not via actual speaking practice by the user—on oral grammar, language functions, cultural appropriateness or conversational strategies. In an application of the multiple choice format to "interactive" video, the user is cued by a video scene and asked to select the culturally appropriate form from among audio answer choices. Such an exercise provides a potentially interesting format for building listening skills in the context of considerations of cultural appropriateness.

An audio item may cue a multiple-choice listening comprehension exercise or provide data for inferring something about the situation in which the item occurred—for example, (1) the topic of conversation, (2) the relationship of two speakers, (3) the time of day, or (4) the location of the conversation. The inference can be based on several types of information which must be extracted from the audio signal, such as the occurrence of certain grammatical forms, the use of certain expressions, and the speaker's voice quality and intonation. With the aid of the computer, such a listening exercise can be individualized in various ways, e.g., by varying the timing of items or the length of the stretches of discourse used as cues. This type of activity is valuable for showing how manipulation of the mechanical characteristics of speech contributes to the interpretation and the construction of meaning.

De Quincy (1986) classifies the facilitative roles which the computer takes on in different types of software as shown in Figure 2. In each case, the computer provides an environment for memorable input, interaction and communicative practice. All of these roles are relevant to the speech-based curriculum, and each of the program types shown can be adapted for use in speaking and listening exercises. Indeed, virtually any computer activity can become an environment for speaking when two or more students work together on one terminal. With the addition of audio prompts, almost any type of program can also offer a focused listening dimension.

The role of the computer as a facilitator of interaction in language classes is fairly well-known and well-accepted by those who have worked with computers in language classrooms (see, for example, Ahmad, Corbett, Rogers and Sussex, 1985; Baltra, 1984; Rubin, 1984; Stevens, 1986; Wyatt, 1984a,c). Yet very little developmental

PROGRAM TYPE	ROLE FACILITATOR/STIMULATOR					
	Opponent	Task Setter	Manipu-lator	Enabler	Simulator	Environ-ment Provider
Manipulative	● ● ● ● ●	○ ○ ○ ○ ○				
Problem Solving	○ ○ ○ ○ ○	● ● ● ● ●				
Text Recon-struction		○ ○ ○ ○ ○	● ● ● ● ●			
Text Construction			○ ○ ○ ○ ○	● ● ● ● ●		
Simulation					● ● ● ● ●	○ ○ ○ ○ ○
Adventure					○ ○ ○ ○ ○	● ● ● ● ●

Figure 2. Different roles that can be generated with six major software types.
(The ● ● ● ● ● represent an area of definite focus for that type of software. The ○ ○ ○ ○ ○ represent an area of possible focus.)
From De Quincy, 1986, p. 6

energy has gone into the design of software intended to elicit certain types of interactions or responses from language learners. One of the most fruitful areas for software development at the present time would seem to be the design of programs which elicit and practice specific types of interactions or language forms—e.g., through task-based learning activities or through the juxtaposition of two or more symbol systems in a certain type of activity, as exemplified by Dickson's "referential communication game" and the variations on it described here.

Research and development is also needed into the most productive ways of allying computers to peripherals, especially those which allow speaking or listening capabilities in language instruction. Several directions for such research and development efforts are outlined in the next section. There the discussion moves to a focus on computer applications in non-interactional speech-based activities which train the mechanical aspects of production and perception.

Training of Production and Perception of Speech in Non-Interactional Formats

Typically, the mechanical aspects of speech are trained in non-interactional speech-based activities involving individual or choral repetition in a class, language laboratory, or tutoring session. The usual mode of instruction employs live or taped models for imitation and feedback on performance. The disadvantage of working on pronunciation in the whole-class format is that the feedback cannot be continuous and individualized. The tutorial situation, in contrast, allows for continuous and individualized feedback, but is entirely inefficient from the viewpoint of an instructor who has to give separate lessons to a large number of students needing help in speaking and listening.

Unlike traditional ways of training pronunciation, the computer offers unique ways to juxtapose symbol systems to provide analysis and feedback on individual users' output. Kalikow and Swets (1972) represent an early attempt to apply computers to the generation of "target," or canonical, phonemes in second language acquisition. The type of device which they used, and which has been adapted and widely used since, analyzes a user's production of certain sounds and then compares the production to the target positions of those phonemes. The comparison may be made visually by means of locating the user's production, inputted by microphone or audiotape, within a vowel triangle or trapezoid, or some other geometrically organized **phonetic space** intended to model the shape of the vocal tract. Or, a graph may show the percentage of overlap between the user's acoustically analyzed output and the acoustic properties of the stored target. In a game challenge feature, the user is prompted in one experimental version of this type of program to make a bar graph reach as close as possible to the top of the screen. The height of the bar graph indicates the percentage of overlap of the user's production as compared with the stored representation of that sound.

This kind of computer capability has great creative potential, though it suffers from certain problems related to the accuracy of the stored targets and the matching of these to the inputted speech.

In normal conversation, many phonemes do not in fact reach their canonical articulatory points, or targets, and indeed, there are no precise targets which are relevant in all cases. Rather, phonemes exhibit a certain range of variation and are better represented by certain regions of an articulatory space rather than specific points. To make matters more complicated, even in a given language or dialect, there may be more than one articulatory region which applies to a certain phoneme, that is, there may be more than one acceptable way of producing a native-sounding phoneme. Given this range of variation, there are problems inherent in trying to "train" the computer to analyze a particular speaker's phoneme productions in comparison to a stored template or set of parameters. It is difficult to create a template which will represent the flexibility of targets inherent in speech production and which can at the same time be used as a basis for reliably judging how close a speaker comes to native-like accuracy in a particular context when producing individual sounds.

Nevertheless, this capability can usefully represent in visual form the difference between native speakers' production of certain phonemes in different contexts, giving a non-native user visual access to the range of variation possible in the phonemes of a second or foreign language. This range of variation differs from language to language (see Delattre, 1981), so that a visually contrastive view of the range in the first and second language may be enlightening for the learner. A visual representation of phonetic quality in different communicative contexts also provides a research environment for eventually being able to design accurate and representative graphic models of phonetic space and for improving the templates used for analyzing speech input. The key to improvements in this technology, I believe, is a shift in focus from individual phonemes to suprasegmental properties as the basis for speech analysis, recognition and training.

The visual modality gives language learners and teachers a new way of perceiving aspects of pronunciation. A variety of types of visuals exist or can be created to model characteristics of the speech signal analyzed by the computer in conjunction with peripheral equipment such as an **oscilloscope**, which represents certain properties of the speech wave. One device, for example, represents vocal pitch (fundamental frequency) or stress (intensity) as an oscillating line across the computer screen. Another represents the speech signal generated by the user as a colorful set of bar graphs which can be matched to a stored template. Still another represents some acoustic properties of the speech signal as a kind of cityscape of buildings of different heights. Already in development are devices that match speech input to continuously varying graphic displays of tongue movements, lip shapes, and jaw opening. In addition, we can expect that software developers will think of creative variations on such displays and novel ways to apply the knowledge gained from analyzing such visuals to lesson design for language learning.

One speech analytic device provides a visual display of pitch and/or intensity based on input from a microphone or other audio source such as a tape player. The display is in the form of a slightly simplified acoustic contour. When interfaced with a personal computer, this type of device can also calculate a number of statistics based on fundamental frequency. Both the visual, graphic display and the statistics can be printed out to create a permanent record for pedagogical, research or testing purposes. It is also possible with the aid of a computer to store one contour on half the screen, then display another contour on the other half of the screen. This allows for the possibility of visually comparing the performance of a student to, for instance, the teacher's performance stored in the computer. The computer allows for designing and storing lessons that incorporate the visual displays and of utilizing a peripheral device to provide speech accompaniment.

Several studies (de Bot 1983; de Bot and Mailfert, 1982; James, 1976) have shown positive effects for visual training of intonation using computer-generated visual displays. A strong positive effect in both perception and production was found for only 12–15 minutes of audiovisual training of intonation using computer-generated visuals for French and Dutch learners of English (de Bot, 1983; de Bot and Mailfert, 1982). In the training, students were exposed to an overview of the various components of pitch contours consisting of:

1. direction of pitch change (rise, fall, level)
2. range of pitch change (difference between high and low levels)
3. speed of pitch change (how abruptly or gradually the change happens)
4. place of pitch change (in sentence, word, or syllable)

(from de Bot and Mailfert, 1982; adapted from 't Hart and Collier, 1975)

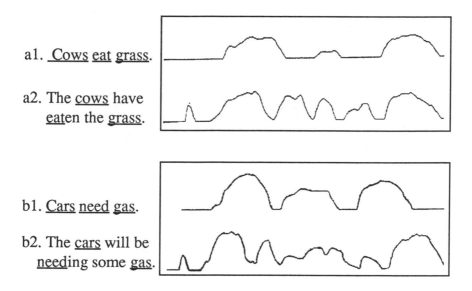

al. <u>Cows</u> <u>eat</u> <u>grass</u>.

a2. The <u>cows</u> have <u>eat</u>en the <u>grass</u>.

b1. <u>Cars</u> <u>need</u> <u>gas</u>.

b2. The <u>cars</u> will be <u>need</u>ing some <u>gas</u>.

Figure 3. Intensity Contours Indicating Similarity of Duration for Sentences Containing Three Main Stresses (marked by underlining), with (2) or without (1) Additional Weakly Stressed Syllables. (Sentences from Woods, 1979)

In his 1983 experiment with Dutch learners, de Bot found that students who received only auditory feedback in the form of repetitions of their own performance did not repeat as much as those who received both auditory and visual feedback. He concluded that the subjects receiving visual feedback were more motivated to continue trying to pronounce a sentence because they received continual feedback on their performance in the form of a visual representation which they could compare with the correct contour. Thus, we can

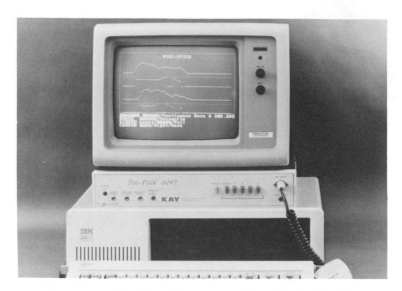

Figure 4. The Kay Elemetrics Visi-Pitch Machine

assume that the visual image of the contour not only represents auditory information in a different modality, thereby making it easier to comprehend or remember, but also provides affective feedback or reinforcement, thereby making it easier or more interesting to attain the target production.

This kind of speech analysis equipment has been widely used in working with hearing-impaired students, stroke victims and others who do not have full hearing or speech capability. However, such equipment has hardly been applied yet to second or foreign language teaching. Among the applications which can be envisioned, besides the tutorial mode which has been most widely used with clients of speech therapists, are uses for perceptual training of groups of second- or foreign-language students or teachers using a large-screen or networking capability in a classroom or language laboratory. It may also be possible eventually to deliver individual feedback and training on production in an efficient way using this type of equipment in a language laboratory setting in which student monitors are all connected to the teacher's computer. Another use (see Esling, 1986), is as a tool for phoneticians or students of phonetics to analyze digitized speech samples contained in a phonetic data base.

There are many ways of applying speech analysis in the training of production and perception of speech. Figure 3 gives an example of a type of contrast in visual displays which might be useful for a student of English and which could provide the basis for a lesson to work on stress and rhythm. The visual displays, which were generated by the Kay Elemetrics Visi-Pitch machine shown in Figure 4, model the fact that the timing of a sequence of stressed syllables or words (indicated by the period of the intensity contour) shows a tendency in English to be approximately constant, even when several unstressed syllables or words are added between the stressed syllables or words. Computer-generated speech displays of other types could provide the basis for graphic representations of, or lessons on, the phenomena of linking, contraction and other forms of reduction and phonological processes associated with fluent speech (Bjarkman, 1986; Hieke, 1984). Lessons in both production and perception of reduced forms could make effective use of computer-generated or computer-inspired visual displays.

Applications of visuals to the training of production and perception do not have to rely on complicated algorithms or expensive peripheral equipment. A simple application could involve an indication on the screen of appropriate groupings of words in a running discourse, showing the places where linking and pausing would be likely to occur in native speech. As another element, text could be added to the screen with appropriate timing of clusters of text between potential pause-points. The student would try to match the timing and groupings indicated on the screen by speaking the text as it is appearing on the screen. An indication of rhythm and pitch could also be part of the display, which might be synchronized with a tape recorder for working on perception of rhythm or for helping to synchronize the student's productions with the visual displays.

The applications of computers in training production and perception which have been described above are in some cases not new, though they do not seem to be as widespread as other kinds of computer applications to language instruction. In other cases, the uses described above, while not yet implemented, are only a short step beyond the types of computer-assisted language instructional software and peripheral devices available at the present time. On the basis of the uses described above, applications of computers to proficiency testing and language acquisition research can be envisioned which make use of similar computer capabilities. As language testers and researchers continue to search for ways to achieve the greatest reliability and validity of results, these two areas of computer application are likely to receive considerable attention in the future. The next section explores some ways in which oral or aural proficiency testing and acquisition research might benefit from use of computers (see also Alderson, 1986).

6.4   Applications to Proficiency Testing and Language Acquisition Research

Features of Computer-Driven Tests of Speaking and Listening Proficiency

A computer-driven test in which students work at individual terminals has many advantages in terms of both standardization and individualization. A listening comprehension test can be computerized by storing test instructions and test items of one or more sentence(s) as digitized speech. This digitized speech can then provide audio-cueing during test administration. Computerization of testing helps to eliminate threats to reliability and validity related to unequal testing conditions caused, for example, by poor acoustics in the test facility or differences in test administration by different testers. In addition to the fact of individual access to the stored instructions and test items, this kind of testing system has the advantage of automatic recordkeeping and scoring of items. It also offers the possibility of customized pacing of the test, which up to now has not been feasible in a standardized listening comprehension test.

A self-contained computerized testing system makes possible additional aspects of testing which are difficult or impossible to realize without such a resource. As a radical example, there is the potential for branching during testing, to gear the difficulty level of items up or down according to the student's performance on earlier items. Another radically new application to testing might be the possibility of students asking for hints or repetitions of certain items, with the computer keeping track of these requests and weighing the number of hints or repeated items into the final score. In this way, students at widely varying proficiency levels can comfortably take the same computerized test, though each might be branched to different sections of the program.

A computer-driven test that makes use of digitized speech stimuli, which can be easily and quickly accessed in any sequence, opens up exciting possibilities for individualization. For example, an audio test item might ask the test-taker to identify a certain situation based on a variety of lexical, syntactic and phonological cues in a stimulus (one or more sentences) which has been extracted from a longer discourse. At the student's request, the program might supply progressively more context in the form of additional parts of the discourse from which the excerpt has been taken. The student's score would be partially determined by the amount of discourse requested to help identify the stimulus.

A computer-driven system with speech access can also be used to test listening acuity or perceptual accuracy rather than listening comprehension. For example, digitized pairs of items might be judged by the user as "same" or "different." These might include the traditional types of "minimal pairs" as well as what might be termed "maximal pairs"—whole phrases or sentences which are difficult to distinguish under conditions of rapid, fluent speech and impossible to test under less than ideal testing conditions. For example, the audio stimulus might be "Susan and Sam don't owe him much," with weakening of *and* to /n/, loss of final /t/ in *don't*, linking between the /n/ in *don'* and the initial vowel of *own*, and loss of initial /h/ in *him*. The answers for matching such a spoken item to its graphemic representation might be:

(a) Susan and Sam don't own much.

(b) Susan and Sam don't know much.

(c) Susan and Sam don't owe much.

(d) Susan and Sam don't owe him much.

Clark (1986) reports on a project coordinated by the Center for Applied Linguistics to develop a "semi-direct" test of spoken language proficiency in which speakers respond on tape to a sequence of tape-recorded stimuli that approximate as closely as possible a live interview situation. This testing procedure, which is a major step towards automated, standardized assessment of oral ability in a foreign or second language, could easily be adapted for computerization, making use of tape-recorded or digitized speech samples synchronized with screen instructions to replace test booklets. In a computerized speaking test, both low-level and advanced students could adjust the time periods between test items to provide a comfortable pace. Typically, in designing an audio-based test of language production, there has been a problem in trying to give advanced students sufficient time to express all that they can express before going on to the next item (see discussion in Clark, 1986), while not leaving low-level students waiting for a relatively long period for the next test item after they have finished responding to the previous item. Hence, computerization eliminates many of the problems encountered in testing without computers, making the whole process of testing easier for tester and testee, while opening up many new avenues for changing testing procedures to make tests more reliable and potentially more valid as well.

With some extension and modification, this kind of testing system can become an environment for testing or diagnosing listening and speaking skills all within the same system. For example, a student might be asked to judge whether a certain pair of items presented in audio form are the same or different. After making a decision and registering an answer, the student would then be prompted by the computer to pronounce the pair. The student's production would be recorded and stored for analysis and comparison with the score for the related listening item. If the student correctly judged the item pair but incorrectly "repeated" the pair—either making a distinction where none occurred or pronouncing two different items the same—then this would indicate that the student's problem is not in perceiving a certain similarity or distinction but rather in producing it. Other aspects of listening and speaking skills, such as speed of reception and production, can also be tested with the aid of the computer.

In addition, speech analytic capabilities make possible analysis of the production of longer stretches of speech generated, for example, by reading aloud, describing pictures or giving directions related to problems or graphic displays shown on the screen. Or, a set of audiotaped questions, remarks or other types of cues can be used to elicit certain structures, functions, culturally appropriate speech behavior or types of interaction with the computer. Use of interactive video to establish a realistic setting for the test items may alleviate some of the problems cited by Clark (1986) in semi-direct testing, particularly face validity. The computer can then provide a diagnosis and training of the mechanical aspects of the particular meaningful language. In this way, the computer creates an environment in which meaningful and mechanical aspects of language can be related.

Combining Assessment, Training and Research in a Computerized System

Training and testing can readily be combined within the same computerized system. For training purposes, these types of systems offer the possibility of individualized feedback and branching options, both under the control of the machine and under the control of the student. In the Training mode, the program might offer running or user-accessed on-line feedback on production in the form of tutorials, graphics or comments based on a componential analysis of fluency (Hieke, 1985) such as "Too Slow," "No Linking," "Too Many Pauses," "Insufficient Variation in Pitch," etc. This type of feedback can be seen as analogous to that provided by text analysis programs for written language.

Besides the uses of speech analytic equipment for research on the characteristics of different languages or types of discourse, this equipment can also be used to measure the gradual change in a student's phonetic space in learning a new language (see Flege, 1981, for a theoretical foundation) and the student's improvement in speaking and listening skills over time. Indeed, the computer can provide a self-contained system combining training, testing and research in the development of pronunciation and listening proficiency. In one aspect, such a system can measure the effect of different types of training engaged in by students who work on the computerized lessons. In another aspect, records kept on individual students can help to characterize in detail the stages that learners pass through in acquiring speech-based skills and the degree to which such an "order of acquisition" might be altered or speeded up by computer-based training. In yet another of its many dimensions, the system can provide research results on the reliability and validity of different ways of measuring proficiency in oral/aural skills (see Molholt and Presler, 1986).

Perhaps the most exciting possibilities combining language training, assessment and research involve two-person interactions which are both facilitated and analyzed by a computer. For example, a combination of screen display, audio output and physical manipulation of keys or keyboard alternatives might be required to perform some kind of cooperative task requiring speaking and listening on the part of two people. While the users performed the task, the computer would analyze their performance. The task could be highly controlled so as to elicit a limited performance from an individual user. This performance could be either a listening response (e.g., indicating which of a pair of items has just been mentioned) or a spoken response to a pre-structured question. Or, the task may be more loosely structured in an attempt to gather a sample of relatively natural learner speech for analysis or for on-line feedback and training of the sorts mentioned above.

Such two-person interactions could be performed by two users sitting at one display screen or by users at separate terminals who were in audio contact with each other at a distance—e.g., in a language laboratory or via some kind of telephonic system, across distances as short as from one classroom to another within the same building or as great as from one continent to another. Language lab applications might involve an instructor acting as the conversational partner to each of the students for training or testing purposes. It is possible also to set up the electrical connections in lab booths so that individual students could be paired to work on the same software interactively while remaining in audio contact.

These kinds of uses come very close to applications of computers in situations of "free conversation." As such, they may provide directions for future developments in artificial intelligence, which attempts to have the computer approximate as closely as possible to real-life communication. By using the computer to analyze human productions in real or realistic interactions—perhaps especially the developing strategies of those, who like the computer, must *learn* how to interact in a nativelike way—AI researchers may discover new ways of organizing or simplifying information which will improve AI programming. Moreover, such analysis will provide a wealth of data on which communicational strategies succeed and which do not.

6.5   Conclusion

We have already begun to apply computers to the creation of learning environments for the development of interactional skills in the speaking and listening curriculum. In addition, computers are beginning to be used in effective ways to train and to analyze performance. We are moving closer to realizing Leather's (1983) conception of:

> computer-managed pronunciation training which makes use of synthetic as well as natural speech models, which processes learners' productions to provide visual displays of salient features together with an assessment of phonetic accuracy, and which leads the individual learner through a series of perception and production training activities selected according to ongoing performance, while simultaneously compiling a detailed record of progress for teacher supervision. However, it is far from clear how the new technology can in practice best be applied, given the present limited state of pronunciation teaching theory. (p. 212)

In spite of some promising applications, we still do not know much about the ways in which computers can impact on learning and cognition in pronunciation training nor in facilitating language learning in other respects (see Dunkel, 1987, for a brief overview). Even after we have this knowledge, it is not a direct step to determining the uses of computer media which will be most effective for instruction. It is still up to the educator to determine the best way to use the creative potential of the medium of computers, to move this medium out of its " 'horseless carriage phase' in which it [has been] assimilated into existing practices, adopting the contents and tasks of preceding technologies" and into its own phase, in which it will "exert new influences" (Salomon, 1984, p. 8) on education and on society. The potential of the computer to impact on the curricular areas of speaking and listening is vast. It is hoped that the information and ideas offered in this section have provided some fresh directions for the creative exploration of this wide-open field.

Program Development

7 Designing Software for Vocational Language Programs: An Overview of the Development Process

Carolyn J. Keith
and
Peter A. Lafford

7.1 Introduction

While no one will dispute that computer-assisted instruction (CAI) can add an extra dimension to almost any educational situation, CAI is particularly well-suited to the needs of the student who must learn vocational terminology and usage in a second language. Even more appropriate is the use of CAI for the vocational language student who lacks job skills or who has marketable skills but for whom language continues to be a barrier to meaningful employment. Vocational language programs are intended to meet the needs of this language user who is studying a second language with the goal of acquiring not only general linguistic competencies, but also job-related skills. Computer-assisted instruction is available in vocational language courses ranging from Auto Mechanics to Nursing Assistant, Secretarial and other Clerical courses.

Job-related, technical terminology is the primary focus of vocational language instruction. Such instruction addresses very specific needs. Because of the learning difficulties second language students may experience, however, the medium used to present materials to these students has to be flexible enough to allow for variety and stimulation in the learning process. In addition, vocational language students tend to do well in non-intimidating, self-paced learning environments. Microcomputers allow for a high degree of precision, yet they also provide developers with much flexibility in what will be presented and how it will appear. The microcomputer is thus an ideal tool for vocational language instruction.

This chapter overviews the process of developing software which will be effective for a particular audience of students, with specific reference to vocational language courses. The development process includes the following phases: a **pre-design phase**, a **design phase**, and a **post-design phase**. The **pre-design phase** comprises the question of time commitment, choice of programming modality, staffing of the project, needs assessment, survey of available courseware, and planning for overall content of the courseware. The **design phase** consists of creating or compiling subject material, programming the lessons—including tutorials, exercises, tests, electronic glossary, and management systems, if desired—and making decisions about various aspects of the program—including instructional language level, student control, and the design of error traps. The **post-design phase** requires field-testing of the completed lessons, revising or modifying the developed lessons based on the results of field-testing, writing user documentation, disseminating the finished product, and integration of the software into classroom activities. (For a general discussion of the different aspects of the design and implementation process of computer-assisted instruction, see Godfrey and Sterling, 1982.)

7.2   Pre-Design Considerations

Time Commitment

Before embarking on courseware development, it is necessary to determine how much time can be devoted to the entire project from start to finish. Although it may appear at the beginning that the entire process will be neither long nor complex, initial estimates do not usually take into account all of the variables that occur in the development process. Johnson (1986, p. 3) estimates 600–1000 hours of development time for a single lesson. Developers must become familiar with the hardware and software available for CAI development and then determine which are the most suitable items for the particular project. Once hardware and software have been selected, time must be devoted to each of the subsequent development phases.

Choice of Programming Modality

It is difficult for a developer to develop original, sophisticated vocational language CAI concurrent with a full (or even a partial) teaching load. The development of good CAI requires intense concentration that cannot easily be obtained when the developer is also concerned with a variety of other responsibilities.

There are three levels of complexity and involvement in writing the CAI lessons from which developers may choose, depending on the amount of time available to devote to the courseware project. Developers may work from authoring systems, authoring languages or programming languages (see Ch. 1, "Language"). Publishers and computer companies have produced a variety of authoring systems and authoring languages designed specifically for courseware development. Authoring systems are the most restrictive alternative, yet require little or no familiarity with computer programming. A considerable volume of CAI might be produced using an authoring system in the same amount of time as would be needed to learn and begin implementing an authoring language.

Authoring languages provide the developers with a greater degree of flexibility in program design, but they also require either prior familiarity with computer programming or the ability to acquire a basic understanding of programming. For the most sophisticated CAI developers, actual programming languages may be the answer. They allow for a more efficient use of the microcomputer's capabilities and thus a higher level of sophistication in the final product. At the same time, however, they require more technical expertise and a far greater time commitment than authoring systems and languages.

Staff Composition

Careful consideration should be given to selecting the staff that will contribute to a courseware development project. The required level of expertise with microcomputers and computer programming will depend on the method chosen to develop the courseware. With authoring systems and languages, a minimal level of programming experience among the support staff—and a willingness to learn—is all that is needed at the outset. Whatever the primary staff composition, it may be necessary or desirable to bring in consultants at various points to review and evaluate the materials (see below).

In addition to the technical considerations in staff selection, professional experience in vocational language instruction and methodologies is also important. Development teams comprised solely of educators risk producing educationally sound but technologically uninteresting courseware, much of which does not represent a great advantage over written work. On the other hand, programmers working without educators risk producing technologically exciting programs which are not educationally sound. If the project leader is an educator, the staff should include at least one individual with computer experience. Likewise, if the project leader is a technician, one member of the staff should be an educator with experience in the courseware field. Johnson (1986, p. 4) suggests a three-person development team consisting of a **subject-matter expert**, a **programmer**, and an **editor**.

Needs Assessment

A needs assessment is necessary to ensure that the final product will be applicable to the educational programs and student audiences for which it is intended. From a broad-based needs assessment that includes the immediate user population as well as those in other vocational programs, the developers find ways to best design the courseware for the immediate population of a particular course or school as well as the larger user population. A survey of vocational institutions provides valuable information on the type of hardware available to other institutions and on vocational language educators' needs for computer-assisted instruction. Results of this type of survey influence the direction vocational language developers will take to ensure that their courseware is appropriate to a broad range of vocational language programs.

Survey of Available Courseware

As part of the pre-design phase, the developers need to survey as wide a range as possible of the available educational software to find out what the strengths and weaknesses of different programs are. Careful examination of available courseware and reading of critical reviews of educational software will give the developers a better idea of how to design courseware that is both interesting to the user and educationally sound.

Courseware Content

Of special concern to vocational language CAI developers is the intended scope of the courseware content. The primary goal of vocational language instruction is to teach technical and sub-technical terminology pertinent to the student's chosen vocation. Vocational language instruction does not aim to teach the "how-to" of the vocation. Rather, it concentrates on teaching students the terminology that they will need to communicate in the job-specific language of their occupation. It is difficult, however, to teach word meanings without tying them to vocational course content. To completely eliminate all references to the "how-to" would risk diminishing the meaningfulness of instruction. Therefore, it is necessary to decide, before designing the software, to what extent vocational course content will be included.

It is appropriate to focus the content on the function of technical terms in the vocational area, accompanied by examples of the lexical items in context as they might be used on the job. Courseware test questions can focus on determining the student's understanding of the technical terminology without requiring in-depth knowledge of how the lexical items are used in the larger vocational field. This level of understanding can be provided later on in the student's content-specific vocational courses.

7.3 Design Phase

Once the questions in the pre-design phase have been thoroughly examined and answered, it is possible to move on to the initial design phase of the development process. It is here that the software developers conceptualize what they want as a final product. Decisions must be made about lesson content and organization, language, and overall program structure before embarking on the actual programming.

Creating or Compiling Subject Material

Having identified the range of content that the lessons will include, developers must create or determine sources of lesson material. Unless the subject matter has never before been dealt with in an instructional setting, it should not be necessary to create all the materials from scratch. Sources ranging from vocational textbooks to computerized text analyses of these textbooks yield material and vocabulary to be considered for inclusion.

On-site visits to work sites allow the development team an opportunity to familiarize themselves with the working environment relevant to the population for whom the courseware is intended. First-hand observation allows for notetaking, drawing, photographing, or even videotaping the visits. These media records can then form the basis for creating realistic graphics and situations in the software.

In an effort to assure accuracy in the content of the materials being developed, it is wise to have the participation of subject-area experts (either practicing professionals or vocational instructors) to review the materials before time is invested in programming lessons that may later have to be significantly altered in overall design. In addition, it is important to have the materials evaluated by a professional periodically throughout the development process. There should be provisions in the project budget for consultant fees to cover the expense of hiring an internal or external reviewer.

Programming the Lessons

Initial Presentation

It is at this stage of the development process that the basic structure of the courseware will be determined. Given the dynamic capabilities of the computer, it is not a question of whether or not to include graphics, but rather what kind of graphics will be used, and how they can be animated. The software vendor who dismisses the lack of graphics in a program by explaining that the program is designed for adults who do not need graphics to be motivated to use the software is offering a weak excuse for a weakness in the program. Graphics are extremely valuable in any type of program, whether designed for children or for adults. Whether the developer uses a programming language or an authoring system, the effort invested in learning how to add even simple graphics to the program—using a graphics editor, turtle graphics, or alternate character sets (for description of these devices, see Ch. 1, "Inputting and Outputting Text and Graphics")—can greatly enhance the effectiveness of the CAI.

The initial presentation of the material is perhaps the most im-

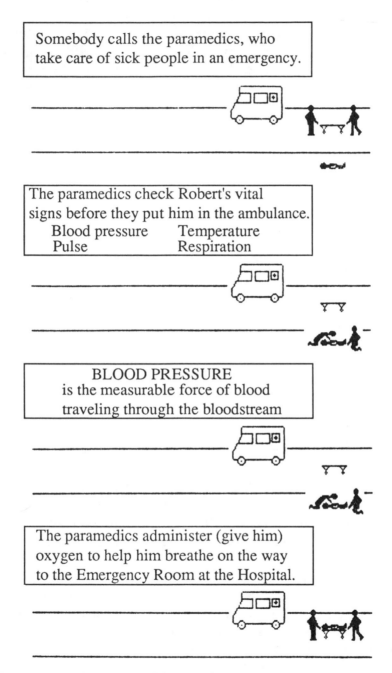

Figure 1. A Sequence of Scenes from an Animated Nurse-Assistant Progam

portant element of the program. Here the computer may act as tutor (Taylor, 1980), engaging the student's interest and motivating the individual to learn the material. As for the fundamental design of the presentation of lesson materials, a look at the kind of information to be presented will yield some insight into the most appropriate presentation format. Developers dealing with lists of vocabulary items easily represented by a graphic might consider a format in which a graphic is accompanied by the word and a simple definition, followed by a sentence using the word in context.

Some content areas, however, do not lend themselves to this graphic-plus-definition treatment. Either the vocabulary is not visual, or the material is procedural rather than conceptual. It might, in such cases, be more appropriate to present the material in a situational context, where animated characters progress through a situation, while a top- or bottom-of-screen textual narration describes what is happening in the graphic display. Figure 1 shows a sequence of scenes which might occur in animated, narrated training courseware designed for a Nurse Assistant vocational language course.

The language of the narration is simplified, and the target vocabulary is either self-explanatory, or restated in paraphrase, thereby teaching the material in meaningful situations. In some cases, videodisc capability might provide options for integrating real-life scenes of the situations illustrated with the computer text and graphics, and narration via an audiotape player or audio output unit utilizing stored digitized speech is also an option (see Ch. 1, "Inputting and Outputting Sound and Video Images"). In conceptualizing the lesson design, it should be remembered that CAI is an interactive medium with the capability to engage the student in manipulation of the lesson material even during the initial presentation. For example, in a clerical course lesson designed to teach how to identify and create abbreviations, students can be directed to identify or suggest abbreviations for words such as those displayed on the screen. The student who participates in the lesson is more likely to learn what is being presented, rather than casually viewing the lesson with minimal involvement and retention.

Exercises

In the next component of a learning module, exercises provide an opportunity for the reinforcement of the material of the initial pre-

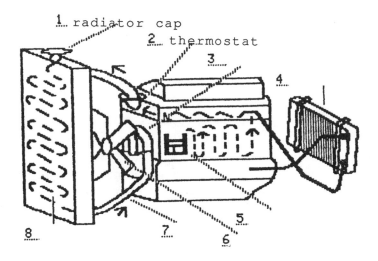

Figure 2. Illustrative Vocabulary Exercise from an Auto Mechanics Program

sentation. Developers normally produce exercises in a variety of formats which offer immediate feedback to the student, and—when the exercises are carefully conceived—motivate the user to investigate or review information which has caused problems in earlier sections. On a wrong answer, the user might be branched, or might choose to branch, to a review screen or into a glossary to look up a missed word, and then return (or not) to the exercise at the point of departure. A second or third wrong answer might prompt the right answer from the computer, so that the student can continue on with the exercise. However structured, the exercises should be designed to function as learning activities that go beyond mere visual input or mechanical manipulation to engage the learner in meaningful activity.

One type of learning exercise is the matching exercise, in which the user types a number or word corresponding to a definition or graphic representation. Matching exercises are relatively easy to design and program, and they can be interesting for the user. Scrambled words, when supported with hints and definitions, can also provide appropriate reinforcement activities that users find challenging and enjoyable. Cloze exercises and more creative exercise formats involving graphics manipulation are among the many possibilities. Figure 2 is an illustration of an Auto Mechanics exercise in which the user matches, unscrambles or types in the lexical item which corresponds to one of the eight labeled parts of an engine in the diagram.

Tests

Another type of learning activity, though with a stronger element of evaluation, can be created in a tests section. To build student confidence, it is appropriate to follow a logical progression of increasing challenge—for example, from true/false to multiple-choice, and then to fill-in-the-blanks items, finally moving on to a free-form application that simulates a real-life situation. For each type of question, it is important to keep in mind the computer's dynamic capabilities. In the true/false section, for example, the user who supplies a wrong answer might immediately be shown why that answer is incorrect, while the correct answer is rewarded with a slightly reworded confirmation of the correct information. In multiple choice item format, wrong choices could be explained. Fill-in-the-blanks answer routines can be carefully constructed to check for anticipated wrong answers or misspellings, and to branch accordingly. A variety of creative and practical tasks can provide real-life applications of knowledge gained in the lessons. For example, a Nursing Assistant program might include a test that requires the user to enter a self-taken pulse over 15 seconds. The program then calculates the beats per minute and responds accordingly.

To distinguish them from exercises, tests can be more structured and restrictive, (i.e., without access to the glossary or review screens), and they can be scored, with evaluative feedback to the user after each group of questions. It is also appropriate to branch conditionally upon completion of a test, either to the immediately following section of the program, or back to the presentation stage or remedial screens, depending on the user's score or preference.

Electronic Glossary

Because these programs are meant to be learning resources, it is desirable that there be a function providing ready access to the vocabulary of the program. One solution is the **electronic glossary**. Designed to be accessible both independently of other program components and from within tutorial or exercise components, the glossary provides the student with definitions of technical terms that may not yet have come up in the lesson or that are causing problems in the exercises. The glossary must have provisions for being able to return a student automatically to a particular point in a program and, upon returning to a previous activity, to re-establish the prior screen, even one that was animated. The electronic glossary must provide a means of dealing with a spelling mistake and of allowing the student to correct it in a way that still permits the student to find the word after it is typed correctly. The glossary is an important component that should be available to keep the user who is motivated to look for extra information from being frustrated by unfamiliar terminology.

Management System

An optional program component is a **management system** that serves a number of purposes for students, teachers, and software developers. Management capabilities are sometimes built into authoring systems, or are functions available in authoring languages. A management system can keep track of which elements of the program each student has completed, allowing individual students to easily resume program use from the point where they left off in the previous session of working with the computer. For instructors, it can track student progress through the programs, recording student responses and test scores. For software developers, an accurate record of student input during field-testing (see below) provides a wealth of data that can be analyzed for correct, and more importantly, incorrect, answers. Should particular wrong answers appear frequently, it would indicate a potential weakness in the material, either in the form in which it has been presented, or in the content of the question.

Instructional Language Level

Remembering the intended audience for the vocational language materials, developers must take care to keep the language as simple as possible. Program control terminology, and especially instructions on running the program, must be basic. As the lesson text is written, it should be subjected to a readability analysis (see Klare, 1974–75, for an overview) to judge the appropriateness of the language for the students who will use the software. There are computer programs which will generate grade-level ratings along standard reading scales based on standardized word lists and syllable counts. The technical terminology will most likely inflate the computed reading level to a point well beyond the reading level of the student, but this is to be expected, given the instructional nature of the program. For a more representative readability analysis, the technical vocabulary may be excluded.

Student Control

Students like to feel as though they are in control of a program when they are operating it, and not that the program is controlling them. Accomplished through the use of menus and consistent, clear program control functions, user control reduces the anxiety level of the student who may feel at the mercy of the computer if there is no way to skip a section, go back a screen, access HELP options, or break out of the program completely. A menu-driven program allows the student instant access to any section of the program by progressing through various levels of menus which present simple, clearly-worded choices in a familiar format. Menu options can be identified either by easy-to-find numbers or by easy-to-remember letters (acronyms or mnemonically-significant letters).

One way of accomplishing user control is through a **floating control module** that provides users with a variety of control options throughout the program, each function available by pressing one letter whenever a prompt appears in the lower right corner of the screen. For example, pressing "B" takes the student back one page or screen, "O" turns the sound on or off, and "?" brings up a HELP screen explaining the kinds of help available to the user. Control options which also appear as menu choices use the same letters to be consistent throughout: "D" takes the student to the Dictionary, or electronic glossary, and "M" takes the student back to the Main Menu. The most likely option, moving the program on to the next screen, can be accomplished by pressing the space bar (which is easier to find and comes more readily to hand than the RETURN key).

It is important to give the student access to on-line assistance throughout the program, particularly on how to control the program. This not only facilitates the running of the program, but serves to allay the student's fears of getting lost or stuck in the program. However, if available options differ depending on the section of the program (i.e., no Dictionary access from the Tests section), the HELP screen displayed at any given point can offer only the options available at that point. To maximize user control, program-use instructions should be kept simple, efficient, and to the point; and the user should never be left "hanging," without an indication of what should be done to continue the program.

Error Traps

No matter how clearly instructions are spelled out, wrong keys will sometimes be pressed accidentally. This is not a matter of wrong answers, which are handled as part of the design of the Test or Exercise sections of the program, but rather of checking that the input is indeed one of the menu or single-character options. When a student presses neither "T" nor "F" for a true/false question, the response should not be counted as a wrong answer or cause disruption of the use of the program. Instead, the student should be prompted to "Press T or F." **Error traps** such as these are simple enough to create by matching student input first for the possible choices, and then for the correct choice. They add to the "user-friendly" nature of the software, and help put polish on the finished product. A tight program will be able to handle virtually all kinds of unanticipated input without "hanging up" or "crashing," and without making the user afraid of continuing, for fear of harming the program or the computer.

7.4   Post-Design Phase

Field-Testing and Revision

To ensure the soundness of the program design, the developers will want to field-test the program, often in some intermediate stage before the full program has been completed. Developers acquire the most useful information by testing the courseware in a variety of educational situations, both "on-site" and "off-site." On-site tests can be conducted with both native and non-native speakers at secondary, college and adult levels. In on-site tests, students are allowed a specified amount of time to work with the program, followed by a brief interview based on a pre-determined set of questions. To optimize objectivity, the student is shown only the keys necessary to control the program; no other instructions are appropriate. The program is then loaded, and the student is told to simply follow the instructions on the screen.

One of the most useful methods of gaining feedback on the field-testing is to observe the students as they use the program. In this way, problems can be noted in the way students work through the program, often information that the student would not think to mention in the interview. In the interview, questions can be asked about the difficulty of the different sections of the program, about how enjoyable the program was to use, and about what the students learned or felt they learned from it.

Off-site field-tests are conducted at the same type of institutions, but without direct observation. Off-site institutions are sent copies of the courseware and instructed to make them available to students in a lab setting, allowing the students to use the software as many times as they wish. Copies of the same questionnaire used in the on-site interviews are sent for the off-site students to fill out when they have finished using the software.

Using these two methods of field-testing, developers obtain valuable feedback that helps to locate the strengths and weaknesses of the courseware. From the information gained, the overall quality of the program can be improved before completing all of the lessons or making the software available in courses.

Documentation

The important thing to remember about documentation is the less required, the better. In the initial design phase, developers should be careful to avoid instructions throughout the program. From the first screen on, program operation ought to be self-explanatory. Nevertheless, before completed courseware is made available to student users, some documentation needs to be written since in many vocational programs, students may use the courseware individually in lab settings, and instructors may not always be available to orient the student to the computer and the courseware. A simple reference guide explaining how to load the program, describing the student control options and indicating where the control keys are on the keyboard removes some of the apprehension students may have about starting to use a new program.

A user's manual explaining the different program functions is helpful as a reference tool for students. It can also be helpful in providing descriptions of data management or data modification capabilities for the course instructor. These options generally require explanation that is best not included on the screen.

The goal in writing documentation is to provide reference tools in a clear, user-friendly style. Many potential users are frightened away from software with detailed explanations that must be read before using the software. The more quickly a student can actually begin to interact with the computer, the more likely the student is to become involved with the program and to use it successfully.

To determine documentation needs, the development team can keep ongoing records of comments about instructions or parts of the courseware that are confusing. Whenever possible, better instructions should be incorporated into the program to address these concerns. These comments also indicate which items need attention in the user documentation.

Dissemination

It is easy to assume that the work is done once the final product and its documentation are produced. This, however, is a false assumption. If the developers intend to make the product widely available, a considerable amount of time needs to be devoted to dissemination of the final product. Software dissemination includes identifying likely users and notifying them of the availability of the courseware, duplicating courseware diskettes to meet incoming orders, providing protective packaging for mailing the courseware, and finally, mailing the copies.

Likely users of the courseware can be found in professional organizations and institutions whose members work with the target audience. For vocational language courseware, appropriate types of institutions include Bilingual Education, Adult Basic Education, Special Education and Refugee Assistance programs. The developers may choose to send courseware descriptions and order forms to this audience in addition to submitting general announcements to professional publications.

At this point, the development process is nearly finished, although not entirely, for software development is never really complete. "Bugs" will emerge in the courseware as users continue to access data in new and different sequences. Also, for any program, there is always room for improvement. The desire to continually "enhance" the courseware can delay its initial release or provide an extension of the development process to produce upgraded versions after the first acceptable version is released.

The threshold of acceptability for release is a difficult one to determine because of the temptation to continue to add "one last enhancement" to the program. Developers need to distinguish between problems that hinder the smooth, sound operation of the program and enhancements that improve the program but are not necessary for the program to run well. The former must be addressed before release of the first version while the latter can be included in subsequent, upgraded versions.

Classroom Integration

As the dissemination and enhancement process develops, questions will arise about how best to integrate the courseware into various curricula. Decisions about such implementation will ultimately be based on two general factors: hardware and software.

Of primary importance to the discussion is the availability of the hardware, that is, what access do the students have to computers? Is there one microcomputer or terminal off in the corner of a regular classroom, or perhaps one with a large monitor in the front of the room for group or whole class work? Are there a few computers in a learning center with open access for all students, or a computer lab of twenty or thirty computers to be used by the whole class? If in a lab, are the computers free-standing or networked? These questions of access are fundamental to integrating CAI into a vocational language program.

How vocational language CAI is actually used depends largely on the specific design and content of the software itself. Of three basic types, courseware can include material that comprises a complete, self-contained tutorial; exercises and activities coordinated with and providing reinforcement of material presented in a class and/or textbook; or supplemental, individual activites not related to a particular course or text, but able to be used in any order.

The self-contained tutorial can be used by students not enrolled in a vocational language class, but who want to pursue vocational training. Such students require access to computers in a lab or a learning center environment, where they will not feel pressured to finish with the computer as quickly as possible so that another student can get access to the only computer in a classroom. It is a shame to compromise the patience of the computer by external time pressures. This is why the computer lab is a desirable option for vocational students.

If such labs are available to students enrolled in vocational language classes, these classes can require outside assignments to be completed on the computer at some point before the next class, much as college language lab requirements are handled. While these materials can be self-contained tutorials, it is more appropriate for vocational language students to use CAI materials designed to parallel and reinforce the class text materials. This type of application is one where teacher-modified commercial materials are put to use to deal with vocabulary identified by the instructor. For example, in an Auto Mechanics class, the student is asked to complete an ignition system game or puzzle in the lab before the next class.

In a computer lab environment, CAI materials can also be provided on an optional basis for those students who feel motivated to use them, either because of interest in the subject matter, or as another opportunity to work with computers. This interest in computers should be considered as a legitimate motivation for language practice, since the language student will most likely be exposed to the language in meaningful contexts, with the added benefit of more computer experience. In this situation, the software used can be coordinated with the text, or it can provide activities of a supplemental, individualized nature.

In the classroom with one computer, CAI cannot provide quite the same patient, individual attention as when computer time is not limited. It is appropriate here to make use of group activities and games where two or three students can work through an activity together, making use of the target language to solve problems or collaborate on answers. The computer might be one station in a series of activities to be accomplished in a class or lab period. In an Auto Mechanics class, for example, groups can proceed around the room where different engine parts are to be examined, diagrammed, and diagnosed for problems, and a related computer activity is to be completed.

Educators can use the one-computer class with a large monitor for presenting simulations for class discussion, again generating situations for language use, both technical and general. In simulation software, a problem is presented for the user to react to, and based on the input or choice selected, the situation progresses in one or another direction. Generally designed for the native speaker, however, commercial programs may require the teacher's assistance in interpreting the problems.

The point to be made here is that the instructor need not feel constrained by the software developers' ideas about how the software is to be used, but might try different applications for given software which can result in an enhanced educational experience for the student.

7.5 Conclusion

The purpose of developing any type of computer-assisted instruction is to enhance each student's educational experience. CAI, especially for vocational language instruction, is a wonderful supplemental teaching tool that can generate renewed enthusiasm in courses for students who do not function well in a traditional classroom environment.

The goal of vocational language software is to create instructional materials that are functional and enjoyable. Well-developed vocational language courseware provides students with the opportunity to move quickly through screens based on information they already know and then to spend as much time as they need assimilating new information. Students control the instructional pace. The content they understand least becomes the content that is emphasized. The program tailors itself to their individual needs. The exercises and tests provide a challenging and rewarding method of reviewing the material and of evaluating their understanding of it. When the time and money are available to support an intense CAI development effort, the results can be most beneficial, particularly for unique educational purposes such as vocational language instruction.

Glossary

algorithm An abstract procedure designed to break a task down into small steps.

applications software Pre-programmed software that allows the user to perform various tasks. Such programs automatically translate the user's commands into the commands of a computer language. Examples of some common applications programs include word processors and data base managers.

artificial intelligence The ability of machines or programs to mimic human intelligence, that is to comprehend, learn and respond in a way similar to humans. Often abbreviated AI. See **expert systems** and **natural language processing**.

Assembly language Programs written in the language of computers, i.e., machine code, consist of a series of 1's and 0's. Naturally, this machine language is hard to understand. Assembly language consists of mnemonic commands (such as LOAD) and numbers that directly parallel machine code, but which are easier for humans to understand. A special **compiler** called Assembler translates Assembly language into machine code.

authoring language A high-level programming language designed specifically for producing educational software.

authoring system A software package requiring minimal programming on the part of the user, which aids in the construction of teaching or testing materials.

BASIC Beginner's All-purpose Symbolic Instruction Code. BASIC is a widely used programming language that is simple and easy to learn.

C A computer language that is growing in popularity. It runs faster than many computer languages without being as difficult to learn as Assembly language. Since UNIX is implemented in C, the popularity of the programming language is likely to grow as UNIX becomes more widely used.

CAI Computer-Assisted Instruction. Covers a wide range of uses of computers for instructional purposes.

CALL Computer-Assisted Language Learning. Any use of a computer to facilitate language learning.

CD–I Compact disc–interactive. Compact discs that can store video, audio and other kinds of computer text and data.

CD–ROM Compact disc–read only memory. Discs principally used for massive text storage.

CPU Central Processing Unit. The 'brain' of the computer, which performs the actual computations.

COBOL Stands for COmmon Business Oriented Language. A programming language for business use. It is useful for information storage and retrieval.

compiler A program that takes programs written in a programming language like PASCAL or C and produces a translation in machine code. The compiled version of a program runs fast, but is hard to manipulate.

computer language A language such as BASIC or PASCAL which can be used to write programs.

courseware Programs designed to help students learn a particular subject.

database A store of information organized in a set framework. The term database is also used to refer to a data base management program, which creates and maintains databases.

disk A form of permanent magnetic storage for computers. Conventionally, the spelling **disc** is used for video and audio storage media.

disk drive A device on a computer which reads information from and writes information to disks.

DOS Disk Operating System. MS-DOS (or PC-DOS) is the common operating system for IBM PCs. Apple DOS is the operating system for Apple IIs. See **operating system**.

electronic glossary An online program containing definitions of technical terms.

expansion boards Components that fit in slots inside the computer and enhance its performance. Expansion boards provide extra RAM.

expert systems AI programs which are able to reason about a limited domain such as medical diagnosis and perform with an expertise similar to that of a human expert.

floating control module Enables a user to give general commands to control a courseware program at any point in the program.

formant frequency A dominant resonance frequency associated with different vowels and consonants.

Fortran Stands for FORmula TRANslation. A computer language used to solve complex calculations.

fundamental frequency The lowest frequency component in a sound, which correlates well with pitch.

grammar checker A program which checks some structural aspects of writing, often including punctuation, repeated words and the use of passive forms.

graphics pad An input device designed for drawing or creating graphics, consisting of a stylus or pen attached to a flat pad. Moving the pen on the pad translates into movements of the cursor on the screen.

hard disks A form of permanent memory storage for microcomputers. A hard disk, which is often mounted inside the computer, has a much greater storage capacity than a (floppy) disk or diskette.

hardware Computer machinery such as monitors, system units, printers, keyboards, etc. The term is often used in opposition to software.

help screen An online system which provides information about commands and general program information.

idea processor An applications program designed to allow the user to write text in the form of headings and sub-headings. Changes in the organization of an outline are very easy to accomplish using these programs.

input/output Data going into or out of the computer. Used as both nouns and verbs.

interpreter A program similar to a compiler that translates a computer program into machine code. In an interpreter, in contrast to a compiler, the translation occurs one instruction at a time and the translation is not saved.

joystick An input device that gets its name from the joystick in an airplane. The computer is sensitive to the movements of the joystick; thus commands can be given by manipulating the joystick.

laserdisc A circular plate used for the storage and rapid retrieval of audio and video material. Unlike conventional disks, laserdiscs utilize laser technology.

light pen An input device shaped like a pen. The computer screen is sensitive to a beam of light emitted by the pen. Commands are given by pointing the tip of the light pen at particular areas on the screen.

LISP Stands for LISt Processing. A programming language popular in the field of Artificial Intelligence. The basic program structure in LISP is in the form of lists, e.g., (add 1 (add 2 3)).

LOGO A programming language related to LISP that is popular in schools. Many LOGO commands are concerned with the manipulation of a graphic-drawing "turtle."

machine language/machine code The internal language of the computer that consists of words made up of 0's and 1's.

mainframe A large, time-sharing computer that supports numerous users simultaneously.

memory The internal memory of a computer is held as RAM or ROM. External memory is stored in various hardware devices including disks and CD–ROMs.

microworld A restricted computer environment such as a simulation of solar systems or Winograd's blocks world. Within the boundaries of a microworld, the user can manipulate parameters or use natural language, for example.

monitor The part of the computer or terminal which contains a screen on which information is presented to the user. A monitor is somewhat similar in appearance to a television set. Other names for it are visual display unit (VDU) and cathode ray tube (CRT).

mouse An input device which can be used to position the cursor on the screen or to give commands. The mouse is manipulated by moving it across a surface and by "clicking" or pressing its button(s).

natural language processing The analysis of a human language by a computer.

operating system Software that manages the storage and retrieval of information on the computer. The operating system is responsible for the various "housekeeping functions" of the computer: keeping order among files and programs, managing the computer's resources (including peripherals) and scheduling its operations. Common operating systems include MS–DOS and UNIX.

oscilloscope A scientific instrument which can be used to display the properties of a speech wave.

paddle See **joystick**.

parallel processing The processing of several units of information at the same time, rather than serially.

parse The rule-based analysis by a computer of a string of words in a computer language or a natural language.

PASCAL A computer language designed to teach good programming techniques. PASCAL is in widespread use in higher education.

phoneme The minimal significant unit of sound in human languages.

phoneme synthesis The translation by a synthesizer of a digital representation of phonemes into sounds.

phonetic space A representation of the vocal tract; a model of the area in which vocal sounds are produced.

PILOT An popular authoring language which is used to develop courseware.

programmed instruction A form of instruction associated with behaviorist models of learning in which a complex task or concept is presented to the learner in the form of a series of small tasks or questions.

PROLOG A programming language popular in the field of Artificial Intelligence.

RAM Random access memory. Internal computer memory which information can be written to, or read from, in any order.

recursion A property of procedures which can repeat themselves indefinitely until a specified condition is met. Recursion is built into many computer languages and is also used in rules in generative grammars. One kind of recursion occurs when a routine contains an instruction which invokes the same routine again.

ROM Read only memory. Information such as operating instructions stored in memory chips. As the name suggests, the processor cannot write information to these chips.

schema A representation of knowledge which is organized to facilitate understanding and recall. Originally applied in AI research, but now also used in research on second language acquisition. Schemas are also called scripts.

serial processing The processing of information in consecutive steps. Contrasts with **parallel processing**.

signal converter A device which on receiving the appropriate instructions from a computer turns a tape recorder on or off.

software Programmed instructions designed to make the computer carry out desired tasks.

source code The original (uncompiled) version of a program, which can be read and altered.

spectrogram A graphic representation of sounds. Time is represented on one axis, frequency on another, and intensity is indicated by the density of the ink.

speech synthesizer A device which produces speech based on the translation of a phonemic representation.

spelling checker A program which checks for misspelled words by comparing each word in a file with the entries in an online dictionary.

spreadsheet An applications program that stores a set of data in grid form and allows the user to carry out calculations on the data.

style checker A program which analyzes a text for potential style problems such as the use of vague words and sexist language.

stylus A pen-like instrument that is used in conjunction with a **graphics pad.**

thesaurus Utility which provides the user with potential synonyms for a word.

touch-screen An input device found on some computers. Commands may be given to the computer by touching different parts of the touch-sensitive screen.

turtle A large triangular cursor which is used to draw shapes on the screen via LOGO or a LOGO-like program. Hence "turtle graphics."

UNIX A powerful operating system developed at Bell Laboratories.

utility A house-keeping program that performs a task which makes the computer easier to use. Utilities may include sorting or file conversion programs.

voice prints See **spectrogram.**

word processor An applications program that helps with the mechanics of writing text.

Bibliography

Abraham, R. G. 1985. Field independence-dependence and the teaching of grammar. *TESOL Quarterly 19*, 689–702.

Abdulaziz, M., Smalzer, W., and Abdulaziz, H. 1985. *The computer book: Programming and language skills for students of ESL.* Englewood Cliffs, NJ: Prentice-Hall.

Addams, S. 1985. if yr comptr cn rd ths ... Software companies mobilize their syntax as the parser war heats up. *Computer Entertainment 25–27*, 76–77.

Ahmad, K., Corbett, G., Rogers, M., and Sussex, R. 1985. *Computers, language learning and language teaching.* Cambridge: Cambridge University Press.

Alderman, D. 1978. *Evaluation of the TICCIT computer-assisted instructional system in the community college.* Research report. ERIC ED 167 606.

Alderson, J. C. 1986. Computers in language testing. In Leech, G., and Candlin, C. N. (eds.), *Computers in English Language Teaching and Research*, 99–110. New York: Longman.

Allen, J. 1987. *Natural language understanding.* Menlo Park, CA: Benjamin Cummings Publishing Co., Inc.

Anandam, K., Kotler, L., Eisel, E., and Roche, R. 1979. *RSVP: Feedback program for individualized analysis of writing.* Research report. ERIC ED 191 511.

Badgett, T. 1984. Computer talks back: new Sidecar gives PCjr human voice, ability to record. *PCjr Magazine 1*(9), 64–66.

Baltra, A. 1984. An EFL classroom in a mystery house. *TESOL Newsletter 18*(6), 15.

Barlow, M. 1987. *Working with computers: Computer orientation for foreign students.* Stanford, CA: Athelstan.

Barrutia, R. 1985. Communicative CALL with artificial intelligence: Some desiderata. *CALICO Journal 3*(1), 37–42.

Bean, J. C. 1983. Computerized word processing as an aid to revision. *College Composition and Communication 34*, 146–148.

Beard, M., Bar, A., Fletcher, D., and R. C. Atkinson. 1975. *The improvement and individualization of computer assisted instruction.* Final report. ERIC ED 112 951.

Benesch, S. 1987. Word processing in English as a second language: A case study of three non-native college students. Paper presented at Conference on College Composition and Communication, Atlanta GA. ERIC ED 281383.

Bensoussan, M. 1986. Beyond vocabulary: Pragmatic factors in reading comprehension — culture, convention, coherence, and cohesion. *Foreign Language Annals 19*, 399–407.

Berens, G. L. 1986a. Using word processors in the ESL composition class. *TESOL Newsletter 20*(5), 13.

Berens, G. L. 1986b. Using word processors in the ESL composition class II. *TESOL Newsletter 20*(6), 13.

Betancourt, F. and Phinney, M. 1988. Sources of writer's block in bilingual writers. *Written Communication 5*, 36–55.

Bjarkman, P. C. 1986. Natural phonology and strategies for teaching English/Spanish pronunciation. In Bjarkman, P. C., and Raskin, V. (eds.), *The real world linguist*, Chapter five, 77–115. Norwood, NJ: Ablex.

Blanton, L. L. 1987. Reshaping ESL students' perceptions of writing. *ELT Journal 41*, 112–118.

Bluhme, H., and Burr, R. 1971–1972. An audiovisual display of pitch for teaching Chinese tones. *Studies in Linguistics 22*, 51–57.

Blum, J., Brinkman, C., Hoffman, E., and Pack, D. 1984. *A guide to the whole writing process*. New York: Houghton Mifflin.

Bolinger, D. 1986. *Intonation and its parts: Melody in spoken English*. Stanford, CA: Stanford University Press.

de Bot, K. 1983. Visual feedback of intonation I: Effectiveness and induced practice behavior. *Language and Speech 26*, 331–350.

de Bot, K., and Mailfert, K. 1982. The teaching of Intonation: Fundamental research and classroom applications. *TESOL Quarterly 16*, 71–77.

Bradley, V. N. 1982. Improving students' writing with microcomputers. *Language Arts 59*, 732–743.

Brazil, D., Coulthard, M., and Johns, C. 1980. *Discourse intonation and language teaching*. London: Longman.

Brebner, A., Johnson, K., and Mydlarski, D. 1984. CAI and second language learning: An evaluation of programs for drill and practice in written French. *Computers and Education 8*, 471–474.

Brown, A. L. 1982. Learning how to learn from reading. In Langer, J. A., and Smith-Burke, M. T. (eds.), *Reader meets author: Bridging the gap.* Newark, DE: International Reading Association.

Buckley, E., and Rauch, D. 1979. *Pilot project in computer-assisted instruction for adult basic education students.* Greak Neck, NY: Adult learning centers, the adult program, Great Neck Public Schools. Final three year report. ERIC ED 197 202.

Burns, H. L., and Culp, G. H. 1980. Stimulating invention in English composition through computer-assisted instruction. *Educational Technology 20,* 5–10.

Carrell, P. L., and Eisterhold, J. C. 1983. Schema theory and ESL reading pedagogy. *TESOL Quarterly 17,* 553–573.

Carrier, C., Davidson, G., Higson, V., and Williams, M. 1984. Selection of options by field independent and dependent children in a computer-based concept lesson. *Journal of Computer-Based Instruction 11*(2), 49–54.

Chapelle, C., and Jamieson, J. 1986. Computer-assisted language learning as a predictor of success in acquiring English as a second language. *TESOL Quarterly 20,* 27–46.

Chaudron, C. 1985. Intake: On models and methods for discovering learners' processing of input. *Studies in Second Language Acquisition 7,* 1–14.

Ciarcia, S. 1984. Build a third-generation phonetic speech synthesizer. *Byte 9*(3), 28–42.

Clark, J. L. D. 1986. Development of a tape-mediated ACTFL/ILR scale-based test of Chinese speaking proficiency. In Stansfield, C. W. (ed.), *Technology and language testing,* 129–146. Washington, DC: Teachers of English to Speakers of Other Languages.

Clark, R. E. 1985. Confounding in educational computing research. *Journal of Educational Computing Research 1,* 137–148.

Cohen, A., and Hosenfeld, C. 1981. Some uses of mentalistic data in second language research. *Language Learning 31,* 285–313.

Collier, R. M. 1983. The word processor and revision strategies. *College Composition and Communication 34,* 149–155.

Curtin, C., Avner, A., and Provenzano, N. 1981. Computer-based analysis of individual learning characteristics. In Hart, R. (ed.), *Studies in Language Learning 3,* 201–213.

Daiute, C. 1983. The computer as stylus and audience. *College Composition and Communication 34,* 134–145.

Daiute, C. 1985. *Writing and computers.* Reading, MA: Addison-Wesley.

Daiute, C. 1986. Physical and cognitive factors in revising: Insights from studies with computers. *Research in the Teaching of English 20*, 141–159.

Dalgish, G. 1985. Computer-assisted ESL research and courseware development. *Computers and Composition 2*, 45–62.

Delattre, P. 1981. An acoustic and articulatory study of vowel reduction in four languages. In Delattre, P., *Studies in Comparative Phonetics*, 63–93. Heidelberg: Julius Groos Verlag.

Dickson, W. P. 1982. Creating a communication-rich classroom. In Wilkinson, L. C. (ed.), *Communicating in the classroom*. New York: Academic Press.

Dickson, W. P. 1985. Thought-provoking software: Juxtaposing symbol systems. *Educational Researcher* (May), 30–38.

Dirven, R., and Oakeshott-Taylor, J. 1984. Listening comprehension (Part 1). State of the art article. *Language Teaching 17*, 326–343.

Dixon, R. 1981. PLATO reaches international students with English lessons. In Hart, R. (ed.), *Studies in Language Learning 3*, 98–112.

Doggrell, J. 1986. The word processor and English composition. *Innovation Abstracts 8* (April 25).

Doughty, C. 1986a. A discussion of Robinson. In *Second Language Teaching and Educational Technology: A State of the Art Symposium*, 47–55. Proceedings of a conference held at the Defense Language Institute, February 6–7. University of Pennsylvania and Defense Intelligence Agency.

Dunkel, P. 1986. CALL sessions: A view of the present and a glimpse of the future. *TESOL Newsletter 20*(3), 5–7.

Dunkel, P. 1987. The effectiveness literature on CAI/CALL and computing: Implications of the research for limited English proficient learners. *TESOL Quarterly 21*, 367–372.

Emig, J. 1971. *The composing processes of twelfth graders*. Urbana, IL: NCTE.

Ericsson, K. A., and Simon, H. A. 1984. *Protocol analysis—Verbal reports as data*. Cambridge, MA: The MIT Press.

Esling, J. H. 1986. Micro-computer-based phonetics instruction using the phonetic data base. Unpublished manuscript. Victoria, British Columbia: University of Victoria, Department of Linguistics.

Esling, J. H., and Wong, R. F. 1983. Voice quality settings and the teaching of pronunciation. *TESOL Quarterly 17*, 89–95.

Fischer, O. H., and Fischer, C. A. 1985. Electrifying the composing process: Electronic workspaces and the teaching of writing. *Journal of Teaching Writing 4*, 113–121.

Flege, J. E. 1981. The phonological basis of foreign accent: A hypothesis.*TESOL Quarterly 15*, 443–455.

Flower, L. and Hayes, J. R. 1981. A cognitive process theory of writing. *College Composition and Communication 32*, 365–387.

Freed, M. 1971. *Foreign student evaluation of a computer-assisted instruction punctuation course.* Technical memo 6. ERIC ED 072 626.

Friel, M. 1985. The computer as electronic blackboard. *Journal of Language Studies 2*, 36–41.

Fry, E. 1963. *Teaching faster reading.* Cambridge: Cambridge University Press.

Gale, L. 1983. Montevidisco: An anecdotal history of an interactive videodisc. *CALICO Journal 1*(1), 42–46.

Godfrey, D., and Sterling, S. 1982. *The elements of CAL.* Reston, VA: Reston Publishing Co., Inc.

Haas, C. and Hayes, J. R. 1986. What did I just say? Reading problems in writing with the machine. *Research in the Teaching of English 20*, 22–35.

Hamp-Lyons, E. 1983. Developing a course to teach extensive reading to university-bound ESL learners. *System 11*, 303–312.

Harris, J. 1985. Student writers and word processing: A preliminary evaluation. *College Composition and Communication 36*, 323–330.

't Hart, J., and Collier, R. 1975. Integrating different levels of intonation analysis. *Journal of Phonetics 3*, 235–255.

Hartley, J. R. 1985. Some psychological aspects of computer-assisted learning and teaching. *Programmed Learning and Educational Technology*, 22(2), 140–149.

Helliwell, J. 1986. Optical overview: What's coming in CD-ROMs and WORMs. *PC Magazine 5*(17), 149–164.

Hieke, A. E. 1984. Linking as a marker of fluent speech. *Language and Speech 27*, 343–354.

Hieke, A. E. 1985. A componential approach to oral fluency evaluation. *Modern Language Journal 69*, 135–142.

Higgins, J. 1983. Can computers teach? *CALICO Journal 1*(2), 4–6.

Higgins, J., and Johns, T. 1984. *Computers in language learning.* Reading, MA: Addison-Wesley.

Hughey, J. B., Wormuth, D. R., Hartfiel, V. F., and Jacobs, H. L. 1983.

Teaching ESL Composition: Principles and Techniques. Rowley, MA: Newbury House.

Hunter, L. 1984. Student responses to using computer text editing. *Journal of Developmental Education 8*, 13–14, 29.

Huntley, J. F. 1986. Beyond word processing: Computer software for writing effective prose. *EDUCOM Bulletin 21*, 18–22.

James, E. F. 1976. The acquisition of prosodic features of speech using a speech visualizer. *IRAL 14*, 227–243.

Jamieson, J. 1986. *Cognitive styles, working styles on computers and second language learning.* Unpublished doctoral dissertation. Urbana-Champaign, IL: University of Illinois.

Jay, T. B. 1983. The cognitive approach to computer courseware design and evaluation. *Educational Technology 1*, 22–26.

Johns, A. M. 1986. The ESL student and the revision process: Some insights from schema theory. *Journal of Basic Writing 5*, 70–80.

Johns, T. 1981. The use of an analytic generator: The computer as teacher of English for specific purposes. *ELT Documents 112*, 96–105.

Johnson, C. G. 1986. Time and design constraints of developing multi-branching language instruction. *TESOL CALL-IS Newsletter 3* (December), 1–5.

Johnson, D. 1985. *Using computers to promote the development of English as a second language.* A report to the Carnegie Corporation.

Jonassen, D. H. 1985. Learning strategies: A new educational technology. *Programmed Learning and Educational Technology 22*(1), 26–34.

Kalikow, D. W., and Swets, J. A. 1972. Experiments with computer-controlled displays in second-language learning. *IEEE Transactions in Audio and Electroacoustics 20*, 23–28.

Kenning, M. J. and Kenning, M-M. 1983. *An introduction to computer assisted language teaching.* Oxford: Oxford University Press.

Klare, G. R. 1974-75. Assessing readability. *Reading Research Quarterly 10*, 62–102.

Kramsch, C., Morgenstern, D., and Murray, J. 1985. An overview of the MIT Athena language learning project. *CALICO Journal 2*(4), 31–34.

Krashen, S. D. 1981. *Second language acquisition and second language learning.* Oxford: Pergamon Press.

Krashen, S. D. 1982. *Principles and practice in second language acqui-*

sition. New York: Pergamon Press.

Lambert, S., and Ropiequet, S. (eds.) 1986. *The new papyrus: CD-ROM*. Redmond, WA: Microsoft Press.

Lambert, S., and Sallis J. (eds.) 1987. *CD-I and interactive videodisc technology*. Indianapolis: Howard W. Sams and Co.

Laver, J. 1980 *The phonetic description of voice quality*. Cambridge: Cambridge University Press.

Lay, N. D. S. 1982. Composing processes of adult ESL learners: A case study. *TESOL Quarterly 16*, 406.

Leather, J. 1983. Second-language pronunciation learning and teaching. State of the art article. *Language Teaching 16*, 198–219.

Lewis, R. 1981. Education, computers, and micro-electronics. *T.H.E. Journal 8*(1), 47–49, 59.

Lian, A-P. 1987. Intelligence in computer-aided language learning. Paper presented in the special symposium, Computers in Applied Linguistics: The Decade of the 1980's and Beyond, Eighth World Congress of Applied Linguistics, August 16–21. Sydney, Australia.

Liou, H-C. 1986. *Language use by pairs of ESL students working on interactive computer language programs*. Unpublished master's thesis. Ames, IA: Iowa State University.

Long, M., and Porter, P. 1985. Group work, interlanguage talk, and second language acquisition. *TESOL Quarterly 19*, 207–228.

Lutz, J. A. 1987. A study of professional and experienced writers revising and editing at the computer and with pen and paper. *Research in the Teaching of English 21*, 398–421.

Lysiak, F., Wallace, S., and Evans, C. 1976. *Computer-assisted instruction 1975–76 evaluation report. A Title 1 program*. ERIC ED 140 495.

Mackay, R. 1974. Teaching the information gathering skills. *RELC Journal 5*(2), 58–68.

Madigan, C. 1984. The tools that shape us: Composing by hand vs. composing by machine. *English Education 16*, 143–150.

Marcus, S. 1983. Real-time gadgets with feedback: Special effects in computer-assisted instruction. *The Writing Instructor 2*, 156–164.

Marcus, S. and Blau, S. 1983. Not seeing is relieving: Invisible writing with computers. *Educational Technology 23*, 12–15.

Marty, F. 1981. Reflections on the use of computers in second language acquisition. In Hart, R. (ed.), *Studies in Language Learning 3*, 25–53.

Melendez, E. J., and Pritchard, R. H. 1985. Applying schema theory to foreign language reading. *Foreign Language Annals 18*, 399–403.

Meredith, R. 1978. Improved oral test scores through delayed response. *Modern Language Journal 62*, 321–327.

Molholt, G., and Presler, A. M. 1986. Correlation between human and machine ratings of Test of Spoken English reading passages. In Stansfield, C. W. (ed.), *Technology and language testing*, 111–128. Washington, DC: Teachers of English to Speakers of Other Languages.

Monohan, B. D. 1982. Computing and revising. *English Journal 7*, 93–94.

Moore, O., and Anderson, A. 1969. Some principles for the design of clarifying educational environments. Reprinted in Greenblat, C., and Duke, R. (eds.), 1975, *Gaming-simulation: Rationale, design, and applications*, 47–71. New York: John Wiley & Sons.

Murphy, R., and Appel, L. 1977. *Evaluation of the PLATO IV computer-based education system in the community college*. Final report. ERIC ED 146 235.

Murray, D. M. 1980. Writing as process: How writing finds its own meaning. In Donovan, T. R., and McClelland, B. W. (eds.), *Eight Approaches to Teaching Composition*, Chapter One, 3–20, Urbana, IL: NCTE.

Neuman, S. B., and Cobb-Morocco, C. 1987–88. Writing with word processors for remedial students. *The Computing Teacher 14* (December-January), 45–47, 61.

Newman, J. M. 1987. Online: Improvising with a wordprocessor. *Language Arts 64*, 110–115.

Nichols, R. G. 1986. Word processing and basic writers. *Journal of Basic Writing 5*, 81–97.

Norton, P. 1983. *Inside the IBM PC: Access to advanced features and programming*. Bowie, MD: Robert J. Brady Co.

Oates, W. 1981. An evaluation of computer-assisted instruction for English grammar review. In Hart, R. (ed.), *Studies in Language Learning 3*, 193–200.

Ohala, J. J. 1983. Cross-language use of pitch: An ethological view. *Phonetica 40*, 1–18.

O'Meara, A. 1986. Computers in writing research: Describing writing processes. Paper presented at a conference on computers and writing instruction — Applications and research, August 1–2. Minneapolis,

MN: University of Minnesota.

Onosko, T. 1985. Let there be light: Optical storage — where is it today? *Creative Computing 11*(9), 43–49.

Papert, S. 1980a. New cultures from new technologies. *Byte 5*(9), 230–240.

Papert, S. 1980b. *Mindstorms: Children, computers, and powerful ideas.* New York: Basic Books.

Pennington, M. C. 1984. Review of ALA/Regents grammar mastery series. *TESOL CALL-IS Newsletter 1* 1, 3.

Pennington, M. C. 1985. Review of the teacher/learner interaction series. *TESOL Quarterly 19*, 353–356.

Pennington, M. C. 1986a. A discussion of Robinson. In *Second Language Teaching and Educational Technology: A State of the Art Symposium*, 56–59. Proceedings of a conference held at the Defense Language Institute, February 6–7. University of Pennsylvania and Defense Intelligence Agency.

Pennington, M. C. 1986b. The development of effective CAI: Problems and prospects. *TESOL CALL-IS Newsletter 3* (December), 6–8.

Pennington, M. C., and Richards, J. C. 1986. Pronunciation revisited. *TESOL Quarterly 20*, 207–225.

Perl, S. 1979. The composing processes of unskilled college writers. *Research in the Teaching of English 13*, 317–336.

Phillips, M. 1986. Logical possibilities and classroom scenarios for the development of CALL. In Brumfit, C., Phillips, M., and Skehan, P. (eds.), *Computers in English language teaching – A view from the classroom*, 25–46. Oxford: Pergamon Press.

Phinney, M. 1987. Approaches to computer-assisted writing in ESL composition. Paper presented at the MEXTESOL XIV Conference, Monterrey, Nuevo Leon, Mexico.

Phinney, M. 1988. Computer-based composition and writer's block in ESL students. Paper presented at New Mexico TESOL, Las Cruces, NM.

Phinney, M., and Mathis, C. 1987. Writing and revising with computers in ESL composition. Paper presented at TESOL Annual Conference, Miami, FL.

Phinney, M., and Mathis, C. In preparation. ESL student responses to writing with computers. Unpublished ms.

Pianko, S. 1979. A description of the composing processes of college freshman writers. *Research in the Teaching of English 13*, 5–22.

Pica, T. 1984. Pronunciation activities with an accent on communication. *English Teaching Forum* (July), 2–6.

Piper, A. 1987. Helping learners to write: A role for the word processor. *ELT Journal 41*, 119–125.

Pufahl, J. 1984. Response to R.M. Collier, "The word processor and revision strategies." *College Composition and Communication 35*, 91–93.

de Quincy, P. 1986. Stimulating activity: The role of computers in the language classroom. *CALICO Journal 4*(1), 55–66.

Raimes, A. 1983. Anguish as a second language? Remedies for composition teachers. In Freedman, A., Pringle, I, and Yalden, J. (eds.), *Learning to write: First language, second language*, 259–274. New York: Longman.

Raimes, A. 1987. Language proficiency, writing ability, and composing strategies: A study of ESL college student writers. *Language Learning 37*, 439–468.

Raleigh, L. 1986. Interactive compact discs: The next step in CD technology. *Classroom Computer Learning 7*(1), 46–47.

Raskin, R. 1986. The quest for style. *PC Magazine* (May 27), 189–207.

Reid, J. 1986. Using the Writer's Workbench in composition teaching and testing. In Stansfield, C. (ed.), *Technology and language testing*, 167–188. Washington, DC: Teachers of English to Speakers of Other Languages.

Reid, J. 1987. Text analysis programs: Which ones work? Paper presented at the TESOL Annual Conference, Miami, FL.

Reid, J., Lindstrom, P., McCaffrey, M., and Larson, D. 1983. Computer-assisted text analysis for ESL students. *CALICO Journal 1*(3), 40–42.

Richards, J. C. 1986. Focus on the learner. University of Hawaii *Working Papers in ESL 5*, 61–86.

Rivers, W. 1981. *Teaching foreign language skills*, Second Edition. Chicago: The University of Chicago Press.

Robinson, G. 1986. *Computer-assisted instruction in foreign language education: A comparison of the effectiveness of different methodologies and different forms of error correction.* Final report. ERIC ED 262 626.

Rodrigues, D. 1985. Computers and basic writers. *College Composition and Communication 36*, 336–339.

Rodrigues, D., and Rodrigues, R. J. 1986. *Teaching Writing with a*

Word Processor, Grades 7–13. Urbana, IL: NCTE/ERIC.

Rodrigues, R. J. 1983. Tools for developing pre-writing skills. *English Journal 72*, 58–60.

Rodrigues, R. J. and Rodrigues, D. W. 1984. Computer-based invention: Its place and potential. *College Composition and Communication 35*, 78–87.

Rose, M. 1984. *Writer's block: The cognitive dimension.* Carbondale, IL: Southern Illinois University Press.

Rubin, J. 1984. Using the educational potential of videodisc in language learning. *CALICO Journal 1*(4), 31–34.

Rumelhart, D. E., and McClelland, J. L. (eds.) 1986. *Parallel distributed processing*, Vols. 1 and 2. Cambridge, MA: The M.I.T. Press.

Rushinek, A., Rushinek, S., and Stutz, J. 1985. Relationship of computer users' performance to their attitudes toward interactive software. *Journal of Educational Technology Systems 13*, 255–264.

Salomon, G. 1979. *Interaction of media, cognition, and learning.* San Francisco: Jossey-Bass Publishers.

Salomon, G. 1984. Computers in education: Setting a research agenda. *Educational Technology* (October), 7–11.

Sarracho, O. 1982. The effects of a computer-assisted instruction program on basic skills achievement and attitudes toward instruction of Spanish-speaking migrant children. *American Education Research Journal 19*, 201–219.

Schaeffer, R. H. 1981. Meaningful practice on the computer: Is it possible? *Foreign Language Annals 14*, 133–137.

Schwartz, H. J. 1984. Teaching writing with computer aids. *College English 46*, 239–247.

Schwartz, M. 1982. Computers and the teaching of writing. *Educational Technology 22*, 27–29.

Schoen, J. 1985. When you talk, your PC listens. *PC 4*(5), 122–132.

Schrupp, D. M., Busch, M. D., and Mueller, G. A. 1983. Klavier im haus — An interactive experiment in foreign language instruction. *CALICO Journal 1*(2), 17–21.

Selinker, L., Todd-Trimble, M., and Trimble, L. 1978. Rhetorical function-shifts in EST discourse. *TESOL Quarterly 12*, 311–320.

Sirc, G. 1985. Review of 'The computer in composition instruction: A writer's tool,' Wresch, W. (ed.) In *Computers and the Humanities 19*, 185–188.

Sommers, N. 1980. Revision strategies of student writers and experienced adult writers. *College Composition and Communication 31*, 378–388.

Spack, R. 1984. Invention strategies and the ESL composition student. *TESOL Quarterly 18*, 649–670.

Steinberg, E. 1977. Review of student control in computer-assisted instruction. *Journal of Computer-Based Instruction 3*, 84–90.

Stevens, V. 1984. Implications of research and theory concerning the influence of control on the effectiveness of CALL. *CALICO Journal 2*(1), 28–33, 48.

Stevens, V. 1985. You'd be surprised at how much public domain software you can adapt to ESL and language learning. *TESL Reporter 18*, 8–15.

Stevens, V. 1986. Using LUCY/ELIZA as a means of facilitating communication in ESL. *TESOL Newsletter 20*(2), 13–14.

Stevick, E. 1982. *Teaching and learning languages*. New York: Cambridge University Press.

Sudol, R. A. 1985. Applied word processing: Notes on authority, responsibility, and revision in a workshop model. *College Composition and Communication 36*, 331–335.

Sussex, R. 1987. Author languages, authoring systems and their relation to the changing focus of CALL. Paper presented in the special symposium, Computers in Applied Linguistics: The Decade of the 1980's and Beyond, Eighth World Congress of Applied Linguistics, August 16–21. Sydney, Australia.

Swarts, H., Flower, L., and Hayes, J. 1983. Designing protocol studies of the writing process: An introduction. In Beach, R., and Birdwell, L. (eds.), *New directions in composition research*. New York: The Guilford Press.

Taylor, M. 1986a. In the beginning: CALL at Western Illinois University, WESL Institute. *CALL Digest 2*(8), 4–6.

Taylor, M. 1986b. Presidential Campaign. *TESOL Newsletter 20*(4), 12.

Taylor, R. (ed.) 1980. *The computer in the school: Tutor, tool, tutee*. New York: Teachers College Press.

Tesler, L. G. 1984. Programming languages. *Scientific American 251*(3), 70–78.

Underwood, J. 1984. *Linguistics, computers, and the language teacher: A communicative approach*. Rowley, MA: Newbury House.

Van Campen, J. 1981. A computer-assisted course in Russian. In Suppes, P. (ed.), *University-level computer-assisted instruction at Stanford: 1968–80*, 603–646. Stanford, CA: Institute for Mathematics Studies in the Social Sciences.

Vinsonhaler, J., and Bass, R. 1972. A summary of ten major studies on CAI drill and practice. *Educational Technology 12*, 29–32.

Waldrop, M. M. 1984. The necessity of knowledge. *Science 223* (March 23), 1279–1282.

Wahlstrom, B. 1986. Using video to study computer-supported writing. Paper presented at a conference on computers and writing instruction — Applications and research, August 1–2, Minneapolis, MN: University of Minnesota.

Weizenbaum, J. 1976. *Computer power and human reason: From judgment to calculation.* San Francisco: W. H. Freeman.

Wilks, Y. 1983. Deep and superficial parsing. In King, M. (ed.), *Parsing natural language*, 219–246. New York: Academic Press.

Williams, L. B. 1987. Suggestions for using word processing in the classroom. Paper presented at the TESOL Annual Conference, Miami, FL.

Windeatt, S. 1986. Observing CALL in action. In Leech, G., and Candlin, C. N. (eds.), *Computers in English language teaching and research*, 79–97. New York: Longman.

Winograd, T. 1972. *Understanding natural language.* New York: Academic Press.

Winograd, T. 1984. Computer software for working with language. *Scientific American 251*(3), 130–45.

Womble, G. G. 1984. Process and processor: Is there room for a machine in the English classroom? *English Journal 73*, 34–37.

Woods, H. B. 1979. *Rhythm and unstress.* Hull, Quebec: Canadian Government Publishing Centre.

Woytak, L. 1984. Reading proficiency and a psycholinguistic approach to second language reading. *Foreign Language Annals 17*, 509–517.

Wresch, W. 1982. Computers in English class: Finally beyond grammar and spelling drills. *College English 44*, 483–490.

Wresch, W. (ed.) 1984. *The computer in composition instruction: A writer's tool.* New York: National Council of Teachers of English.

Wyatt, D. H. 1984a *Computers and ESL.* New York, NY: Harcourt Brace Jovanovich; Washington, DC: Center for Applied Linguistics.

Wyatt, D. H. 1984b. Computer-assisted teaching and testing of reading and listening. *Foreign Language Annals 17*, 393–407.

Wyatt, D. H. 1984c. CALL notes: The receptive way versus computers? *System 12*, 293–296.

Young, R. 1983. The negotiation of meaning in children's foreign language acquisition. *ELT Journal 37*, 197–206.

Zamel, V. 1976. Teaching composition in the ESL classroom: What we can learn from research in the teaching of English. *TESOL Quarterly 10*, 67–76.

Zamel, V. 1982. Writing: The process of discovering meaning. *TESOL Quarterly 16*, 195–209.

Zamel, V. 1983. The composing processes of advanced ESL students: Six case studies. *TESOL Quarterly 17*, 165–187.

Zamel, V. 1987. Recent research on writing pedagogy. *TESOL Quarterly 21*, 697–715.

Zampogna, J., Gentile, R., Papalia, A., and Silber, G. 1976. Relationships between learning styles and learning environments in selected secondary modern language classes. *Modern Language Journal 60*, 443–447.

Name Index

Subject Index